How to
Travel the World
on $10 a Day

Will Hatton

Preface

"To travel is a driving human instinct that stretches back to the dawn of time"

After travelling the world for nearly a decade, I can confidently say that backpacking has changed my life beyond recognition. I first hit the road in search of something. I was searching for some kind of purpose or meaning. There were questions that refused to go away... these questions needed to be answered.

For me, travelling on a budget was a quest. A challenge in which I could test myself, identify my weaknesses and work on becoming the person I wanted to be. When I hit the road, I did so with no money, no plan and just a battered tent for company.

And you know what? It was the best decision I ever made.

I believe everybody deserves the chance to travel. The good news is that if you've bought this book, you are within the bracket of people who can make travel a reality. This book is for the broke and the adventurous, for the dreamers and the leaders of tomorrow. A stint of travelling will arm you with more life experience and confidence than any other opportunity can.

This is because travel takes work. Travel takes commitment. If you are to earn your freedom, you must be willing to sacrifice some comforts in exchange for the incredible experiences that await you.

And if you do, the rewards will be life changing.

I've put together this backpacking dissertation so that you can learn from my mistakes and hit the road armed with the tips, tricks and tools you need to travel the world with confidence. I hope that this book can inspire you to travel far and wide, to love often, and to never give up on your dreams. Whatever you want out of life, it is possible.

The path to victory is never easy, but the best road is found in small, actionable steps… and the first step starts now.

Commit to changing your life, commit to getting what you want, believe in yourself, believe in the world, and you will not be disappointed.

Let's hit the road…

Introduction

Let me start by saying...

You did it!
You fucking did it amigo!
You have officially invested in your future, as of right now, today, you have taken the first step towards living a life of freedom, adventure and opportunity.

What that life looks like, well that is up to you. Nobody can teach you how to travel the world indefinitely, that shit has to be earned – but I can show you how to get started.

I am the scribe and the guide (and also apparently a poet). I am here to show you the way, to offer you the tools you need to hit the road and to mix up your life.

Maybe you daydream about ditching your desk. You want to visit foreign lands, try exotic new foods, and live a life of freedom and adventure.

Perhaps you are in between an awesome job and a gorgeous girlfriend and all you want is a simple gap year, a chance to step out into the world and see what's there. Or maybe you're thinking big, and you want to unleash yourself unto the world and wander the planet indefinitely in search of your tribe.

Regardless of *how long* you want to travel, you're here because **you want to travel**.

You've probably read a bunch of travel blogs, scrolled through endless pictures on Instagram, maybe even put some research into your own backpacking itinerary.

You clearly want to travel - and now you have taken an important step.

By investing in this book, you've made a commitment.

You've decided that you are going to travel the world. You've decided that freedom isn't scrolling through your social media apps, convincing yourself that one day you'll pursue your dreams. **You've decided that freedom is about taking action and actually doing something. And, you're right.**

All great journeys start with a single step. Whether you are about to hit the road for the first time, or have simply run out of money and need some next level travel hacks to keep you going, your evolution into vagabond extraordinaire beckons upon the horizon.

And that's why I finally sat down and blasted out nine years of backpacker knowledge into this book. My blog has enough budget travel information to suffocate a small rhinoceros, but I wanted to create something special for those who truly wanted to supercharge their travel-dreams, and turn them into a travel-reality.

You are going to travel the world. I guarantee it.

Who am I?

In case you don't know who I am, allow me to introduce myself.

My name is Will Hatton. I'm a world traveler, online entrepreneur, and I run one of the world's most far flung travel blogs - The Broke Backpacker.

My goal is simple. I've travelled the world, and now I want to teach you to do the same.

I've spent the last nine years mastering the art of budget travel. I first hit the road as a spotty teenager with an Australian bush hat and very little else. I hitchhiked across Europe to Africa, climbed Kilimanjaro and found a part of myself that I hadn't been in contact with before. These days, the spots and the hat are gone but I'm still travelling strong. #travellingstrong

Having been to 72 countries, I've been lucky enough to see and experience a lot.

I've explored the temples of India, steaming jungles in Venezuela, deserted beaches in the Philippines and incredible mountains in Pakistan. I've hitchhiked through Iran, unleashed my inner Samurai in Japan, gotten beyond blazed in Amsterdam, surfed the waves in Nicaragua and experienced thousands of other adventures in between.

Backpacking is my life. To be on the move, to be taking action, any action, makes me happy. I like meeting interesting people. I like being by myself. Backpacking provides me with everything I need to live a life where I am consistently amused, amazed and impressed.

Over the years, through trial and error (and having no god-damn money) I have unlocked the secrets to budget travel.

And it is these secrets, amongst a few other things, that I want to share with you. I haven't written a book before so this is a new experience for me and I have aimed to make this book as simple as possible to get through. I've dissected the art of travel into small, actionable chapters and I encourage you to flip through at your leisure until something captures your eye. I hope that my musings inspire you, encourage you, and most importantly, empower you with the knowledge and tools you need to confidently get on the road!

This book, like travel, has no beginning or end. OK, I'm lying, there is an end…

But before we can get there, we have to start at the beginning.

Me + you + this book = you travelling the world for as long as you want (team-work makes the dreamwork!).

But let me make one quick side point… I'm not here *just* to introduce you to the ten commandments from the high temple of Backpackistan. Whilst I will arm you with the tools you need to travel on the cheap, I want to share something much more powerful than that.

I'm slowly, but surely, going to show you that if you want it bad enough, you can make travel more than a short trip. *You can make travel a lifestyle.*

How Can You Travel on $10 a Day?

Now let's be clear, travelling the world on $10 a day isn't necessarily easy, and by no means is it glamorous. I've traveled on a lot *more* than $10 a day, and believe it or not, I've traveled on a lot *less* than $10 a day.

This book will show you how to travel from an "extreme" budget, to a more "normal" budget and every kind of budget in between.

If you want to travel on $50 a day. This book will teach you everything you need. If you want to travel on $25 a day, this book will teach you everything you need. If you want to travel on $10 a day… you get it.

If you are looking to travel the world on $50 a day, you'll have a lot more options. Higher budget = more breathing room. But if you want to travel the world on $10 a day, there are certain things that you must do!

Travelling the world for $10 a day will require **five things:**

1.   **Travelling mostly to developing nations**
2.   **Travelling slowly**
3.   **Eliminating the cost of lodging through couch surfing and camping**
4.   **Living, eating, drinking, and getting around like a local**
5.   **A willingness to pick up work on the road when necessary**

If you do those five things, you can travel for $10 a day. I know this because by doing those things, I've travelled for $10 a day all over the world.

If you want to splurge a bit more, go for it! Whenever I have money, I spend it. In fact, the money you paid for this book has probably already been converted into beer by now, so thanks for that. Independent travel comes in all shapes, sizes and varying budgets. I wrote this book to show you how to travel the world regardless of your budget.

We have so much to cover.

Let's get started.

$10 A DAY

The five things you must master to travel the world on the cheap

WHERE TO TRAVEL

To travel on the cheap, you MUST venture to developing nations. Asia, Eastern Europe and Central America (amongst others) cost a fraction of their developed counterparts

STYLE OF TRAVEL

To travel cheap, you have to travel **slowly**. By traveling slowly you'll be able to really appreciate the experience and keep costs much lower (not to mention you get more time to relax!)

FREE LODGING

Over time, lodging can be very expensive. To stay under the magic $10 number, you should couchsurf or camp every chance that you get. But get excited - they are both **amazing experiences**

LIVE LIKE A LOCAL

Eat, sleep and live like a local. By utilizing local buses and trains, eating native food, and learning to haggle, you'll be seeing the country as authentically as possible (and cheaply)

PICK UP WORK

To cut the cost of travel you have to be willing to pick up work on the road. There are dozens of ways to make money traveling. Even better, start your own business online

www.TheBrokeBackpacker.com

Chapter Breakdown

1. Let's Talk about Travel
- Finding the time to travel
- Is long-term travel a good investment?
- Dealing with family and friends
- Why you should travel independently
- Overcoming your fears
- It's not always easy, but it's worth it

2. Travel Inspiration
- What do you want out of travel?
- Why you should travel to developing nations
- Should you buy a round the world ticket?
- Why you shouldn't 'do' a country in a week
- Types of backpacking trips
- Epic adventure challenges
- Great journeys of the world
- My two cents

3. Travel Planning – A.K.A Winging it like a boss
- Why you should stay flexible
- Why your plans will change
- Choosing the best time to travel
- Why most travel guides are bullshit
- Handy apps
- Online travel resources
- The backpacker grapevine

- Finding a place to sleep
- Dealing with visas
- Making decisions without getting stressed

4. Finances
- How much money do you really need?
- Saving up money
- Money saving tips
- Making money while travelling

5. Broke Backpacker Hacks 101
- Why travelling broke is the best adventure
- Accommodation 101
- Hostels 101
- Camping 101
- Couchsurfing 101
- Couchsurfing as a safety net
- Squatting 101
- Transport 101
- Hitchhiking 101
- Food 101
- Dumpster Diving 101
- Haggling 101
- Booking online or offline?
- Money saving tips

6. Travel Gear
- Travel light as a feather
- Backpack vs. suitcase
- What you need to spend money on
- Hitching and camping

- Packing lists
- Essentials checklist
- Clothing checklist
- Tech checklist
- Adventure checklist
- Hiking gear checklist
- Toiletries checklist
- Medical checklist
- Documents checklist
- Buying travel insurance

7. Staying Safe on the Road
- The world is NOT out to get you
- Real dangers to backpackers
- Precautions against theft
- Travelling as a woman
- When to run and when to fight
- How to defend yourself
- What to do if you're mugged (or worse)
- Digital security and backups
- The world IS safe

8. Health is Wealth
- Travel workouts to keep you fit
- Health tips
- Why travelling slow keeps you healthy
- Why you should travel with a first aid kit
- Getting vaccinated

9. Making the Connection
- I used to be super shy

Chapter One
Let's Talk about Travel...

It might seem counter intuitive, but before we kick off 60,000 words of budget travel awesomeness, we should ask ourselves...

Why the hell are we even travelling in the first place?

What's the big deal with this whole travel thing? Why does everyone freak out about it?

Why is it that regardless of sex, age, job, nationality, and personal interests - that when you say the word *travel,* everyone seems to light up?

Whenever I ask people, 'if you could do anything, what would you do?'

The answer is almost always the same - 'Travel'.

Shepherds in Pakistan, clerics in Iran, policemen in Myanmar, students in Europe - we all have one thing in common; **we want to travel.**

To travel is to seek opportunity, to seek a better life. For millions of years, humans (and our earlier counterparts) have travelled across this planet in search of food, shelter and mates.

Today, we no longer have to run down a wooly mammoth to get a meal (which is kind of a shame) but we continue to move, we continue to follow our feet and to gaze towards the horizon.

Some people love travelling because of the freedom.

Some people travel to test themselves and to grow as

individuals by conquering their fears.

Others want to escape. Many want an adventure.

Travel can be relaxing. Travel can be intense.

Perhaps the best description of travel is a journey filled with opportunities beyond your wildest dreams.

The power of travel is beyond description. It challenges you. It empowers you. It breaks you. It amazes you. It's a powerful cycle that will teach you more about yourself than any other experience in life can. If you want to know who you are, and want to improve yourself, while living a life of passion - then I urge you to travel. But then, you already know that that is what you want to do.

For me personally, living a life of travel is living a life amplified. It heightens my senses. I feel more alive.

One of my earliest adventures was to India. I was nineteen, by myself and I didn't have a phone. It was scary, but it was glorious. I spent eighteen months hitchhiking, camping and couchsurfing, working on farms, selling weed in Goa and having a ball. I didn't have much money at all but I had an incredible sense of freedom. I could do pretty much whatever I wanted, as long as I was willing to accept a certain level of discomfort. I was hooked.

I knew that further down the line I was going to get sick of being poor in a foreign, and sometimes difficult, country but I also knew that if I could smash through those challenges and roll with the punches, I would emerge as a stronger, more capable, human.

Once you get a taste of travel, you get a taste of that amplification. You see the world in in all of it's incredible colors… and it can be really tough to go back to a life where you have less freedom to be and do what you want.

There are those who dub this feeling *'Wanderlust*, and even though it's arguably the most overused and annoying freaking term in the travel world - it is a real thing.

And it is powerful beyond explanation.

Finding the Time to Travel

Ah. Time. Yes. If I had a nickel for every time I tried to convince someone to travel more and they responded with *'I want to! I just don't have the time!*.... I'd... have a lot of nickels.

And I get it.

Time is the most valuable resource we have. It dictates everything in our lives. This is because our time is limited. Our time is finite. And in terms of our personal allotment of time... it is going to run out.

One day you are going to die.

It's a certainty. Just as much of a certainty that there are going to be more Pirates of the Caribbean movies. One day, scientists might be able to solve both of these problems, but until then death, and Pirates of the Caribbean Eleven are completely inevitable.

So. If it is certain that our time is limited, how could you possibly use it as an excuse *not* to travel?

I understand that we have jobs, families, student loans and the occasional mafia debt - but if you really want to travel, you'll find a way to make the time for it. I've met an incredible array of people on the road, I've met travelers of all ages, from all backgrounds and all walks of life and all of them are making it work, all of them have found the time to travel.

Travel is open to everyone, but not everybody is up to the task. You see, to travel takes work. For some, it's a lot more work than others. That said, with sacrifice and hard work, anybody can travel. I've met an incredible array of people on the road. I've met bankers, bus drivers and receptionists who have quit their jobs and are taking some time out before starting something new. I've met lawyers, lecturers and real estate agents who have negotiated for a few month's unpaid work whilst they explore new opportunities. I've met talented specialists – strippers, web designers and professional poker players – who have discovered that they can pay for months of travel with just a couple of week's work. I've met businessmen, freedom fighters and entrepreneurs who have taken a couple of years off to travel before springing back into the fray. Some of the most successful long-term travelers I have met are those who work seasonal skiing or sailing instructor jobs. Before I earned an income from my blog, I worked dozens of shitty jobs all around the world to pay my way and fund my next adventure. So many people before you have found a way to make it work, to find the time to travel, that the path is very clear indeed. If you love your job, negotiate for time off. If you're any good at your job, you are very likely to be granted it. If you are not granted that time, quit.

Because if you don't make time for travel, you'll regret it. Sometimes we regret the things we did.

But more often, it's the things we *didn't do,* that we end up regretting the most.

When you're on you deathbed, you'll be much more likely to regret *not* travelling the world. You'll regret *not* pursuing your passions. Regret sucks.

Is Long Term Travel a Good Investment?

In my opinion, travelling is one of the best investments you can make. The experience of travel will give you the opportunity to develop a much wider range of skills than if you were to charge straight into a job after school.

Travelling the world is one hell of an experience… and it honestly could give you an advantage in the job market!

Investing in Life Experience

Think about it. Let's pretend you are a hiring manager at a competitive firm. There are two people applying for the same job.

Both applicants have similar grades. Both have similar credentials.

The first applicant is young, and fresh out of uni.

The second applicant graduated a few years ago, but her resume is highlighted by the fact that she just got back from travelling the world solo for eighteen months.

Most often, the competitive edge goes to the second applicant.

This is because companies aren't *just* looking for bright students fresh out of uni. The hiring process (especially in competitive industries) is all about making yourself stand out from the crowd. It's about illustrating your value, not just as a bright student, but as a fully functioning individual!

Hiring managers want maturity. They want world experience. They want people who can solve problems and most importantly, they want people who know how to **adapt!**

World travel teaches you all of these things and so much more. You'll be able to highlight the skills you have learnt whilst travelling; independence, flexibility, negotiation, planning, bravery, improvisation and adaptability. You can mention your newfound talent for budget management and the social skills and empathy you've gained through world experience. World travel teaches you how to tolerate and understand. Travelling the world shows you have patience and determination, and displays that you have the adaptability and willpower to succeed in challenging times.

If you are super stoked about getting a job in a field you've worked years toward - awesome! I'm certainly not trying to dissuade you.

Just realise that travelling the world will not decrease your chances of finding a job, it'll most likely **increase** them.

Remember what we talked about - everyone wants to travel. It's a universal desire! The person responsible for interviewing and hiring you probably likes to travel too. This will get them excited about you. When they are interviewing you, listening to your tales of independently travelling to far flung lands, they're probably going to be impressed and just a wee bit envious.

Travelling the world helps separate you from the crowd while simultaneously demonstrating your life skills and just how much of a badass you are.

Investing in Happiness

I have a question for you...

Whatever job you're invested so heavily in... is it making you happy? Would you rather transport yourself to a far flung land or spend another day hustling at work?

For some of you, the answer may be the latter and that's not wrong. I know that I personally love to get stuck into projects and to work hard – as long as I'm working for myself. The thing is, even if you are a hustler, everybody needs space and time to reflect on their mission and to regroup for the next battle. Travel can offer you that space, that reflective period, that opportunity to work out what your why is.

Travel will introduce you to new experiences, new people and new points of view. Maybe it's time to worry a bit less about investing into your career, and worry a bit more about investing into your personal happiness, growth or whatever you want to call it.

As you continue reading this book you are going to discover an entire subculture - nay! - an entire **universe** of independent travellers living freely and hustling hard on projects that matter to them, rather than projects that matter to a company's balance sheet.

And in this universe of inspirational guys and gals you will find the tools, inspiration, and most importantly the support, to encourage you to take the plunge.

If we established that our time on this earth finite, why spend any of that limited time doing something you don't want to do?

If you're happy with your job, then congratulations, you are already an inspirational human.

But if you are not happy with your job, it's time to try something new and the best place to figure out what to do is on the open road.

Start travelling, and if you like travel as a lifestyle (which I suspect you might) then there will be numerous opportunities to begin investing your personal time into a career that ties you to no timetable or one location (aka being a Digital Nomad).

Dealing with Family and Friends

There are two types of people that are afraid to travel because of family and friends.

1. Aspiring travellers who are afraid of missing their family and friends
2. Aspiring travellers who are afraid of letting down their family and friends

And many people fit into both categories! Let's get into it...

But I'll miss my family, friends, and home...

The first thing I want to say is that if you are intimidated to travel because you'll miss your family and friends - it's all good, everybody feels the same. Our families and friends are the dearest people in the world to us, and because of that, the idea of separating from them for a long period of time is intimidating.

What will I miss out on? What's going to happen when I'm gone? Will they forget me? How do I keep in touch with them? WHAT WILL I MISS OUT ON?!

I emphasize on the last point for a reason - **FOMO**. It's real and it is potent!

I've known many a friend whose deepest darkest fears revolve around what will happen when they're *not* around.

I had this fear myself. Leaving home the first time was scary. I had an OK job opportunity, a hot girlfriend and a dog, his name was Finn, who was the single most important part of my life. Leaving Finn behind was damn hard but you know what; I saw him again, and again, and again. We were all good, he got it.

And do you know what I learned, and very, very quickly?

The same opportunities, or lack of them, remain available for a really long time.

For a long time, nothing changed in my home town.

I guarantee the situation will be the same for you. Don't have a fear of missing out on the menial stuff in your hometown - have a fear of missing out on the awesomeness that is your life!

And please, whatever you do, do not limit your travel aspirations because of a boyfriend or girlfriend (or even worse – a crush) it simply isn't worth it... Once you get out into the world you'll see what I'm talking about, there are literally millions of gorgeous people out there.

If the idea of heading halfway across the world freaks you out, then do not despair - start small and stay relatively close to home.

If you are from the USA, go to Central America! You'll be able to experience an amazing culture and feel a world away, but if you ever want to go home it's just a few hours on a plane!

Living in Europe? Head to Eastern Europe or North Africa.

Aussie or Kiwi? South East Asia is your back yard!

This is a great way to get a taste of travel while having the peace of mind knowing that if you wanted or needed to go home, you're only a few hours' flight away.

But I don't want to let down my family and friends...

Now, the other type of fear of friends and family is not necessarily the fear of missing them, as much as it is the fear of *disappointing* them.

Our family and friends are very important to us, and because of the closeness of that relationship it's interesting to acknowledge that they have a certain hold over us? A certain... *influence*.

As if going against the grain isn't scary enough, friends and family may think you've lost the plot when you tell them you don't want that mortgage, that 9 to 5 job, that car or to settle down.

Change can be hard for people to bite down and chew on.

Your friends and family are always going to think they know what's best for you, but truth be told, they don't.

They don't feel your feelings. They don't sense your senses. They don't dream your dreams. They can't understand the magnitude and gravity of your desires, just like *you* couldn't understand the magnitude and gravity of *theirs*.

Not everyone will agree with your decision, but at the end of the day, many people will tell you that you are taking a big risk; they are simply projecting their own fears onto you.

If you psych yourself up, assert yourself and listen to your own instincts, you're going to be doing yourself a big life-favour.. Do not be troubled young padawan, step forwards, man (or woman) up and take the plunge...

In other words?

It's your life, live it on your terms.

How I Dealt with Family and Friends

If you feel pressure from family to pursue a certain line of work

- let's hug it out, because I've been in the same boat.

Let's go back a few years to a younger, less tanned me...

When I was eighteen, I wanted nothing more than to join the Marines.

It wasn't even that I wanted it. It wasn't even an option. **It was what I was going to do.** There was no backup plan one, two or three. There was be a Marine... or there was nothing. I daydreamed about making a difference, about finding a purpose, and being a part of something much bigger than myself.

I thought it was my destiny, and I would let nothing get in the way of it.

Well, the gods laugh at our plans, don't they?

Fast forward a year and I suffered a pretty bad injury that had me in a wheelchair for a bit. I recovered from this injury, but it completely destroyed any hope or chance I had to join the Marines. After the injury it was simply impossible.

To say I was crushed would be the biggest understatement of the century. I did not take it well.

My parents in all of their love and thoughtfulness were quick to jump in and suggest alternative career paths for me.

Mum wanted me to be a teacher. Dad thought engineering was the best route. They both wanted me to do something *safe*, and something with a good pension, so I could get a foot in on the property ladder and follow in the footsteps of the millions of people before and after me.

They really were trying to help and thought they knew what was best for me.

I was depressed and vulnerable to the influence of others. I felt lost and didn't want to choose my own fate, it was tempting to go with the recommendations of others.

But deep, deep, deep, DEEP down inside... I knew I needed to take control of my destiny. I didn't know how, so on a wing and a prayer, I hit the road and stuck out my thumb. It was a decision that changed my life forever.

My parents took a bit of time to come to terms with my decision to travel around the world without any set plans, but eventually they accepted it. Yours will too.

Why You Should Travel Independently

Independent travel = backpacking without a guide. And it's the greatest form of travel on the planet. This is for a few reasons.

Lower cost

> Independent Travel is far and away the cheapest way to travel. Actually, if you are travelling broke .... It's the only way.

Light travel

> No checked bags. No luggage. It's you, your shit, stuffed in a backpack, taking on the world. End of story.

Unlimited freedom

> When you travel independently you have the freedom to go wherever you want, whenever you want.

Lifelong friends

> Travelling is like speed-dating but with friends, you will meet so many new people every day and you can pick who you do or don't want to get to know better. I have made most of my close friends whilst on the road.

Personal growth

Resourcefulness, adaptability - you'll be forced to make decisions and every time you do, you'll end up a stronger, savvier version of yourself.

For some truly exciting destinations, like Bhutan and North Korea, it's *only* possible to visit via an organised tour so there is definitely a time and a place for tours but, in my opinion, independent travel offers the greatest opportunities for personal growth, unique experiences and new friendships.

Overcoming Your Fears

If you come from a developed nation - chances are your native country media covers the developing world in a certain… light.

And by light I mean evil, cold, **darkness**. Western media portrays developing countries as third world hellholes filled with nothing but murder, assault, kidnappings and revolutions.

And all of that is just so backwards.

Truth be told, in my nine years of travel, I've frequently felt safer in countries like Iran, Pakistan and Colombia than I have in first world countries.

As a traveler, there are certainly things you need to worry about. Travelling to certain areas of the world will absolutely require a certain sense of diligence.

But the chances of something happening to you while backpacking the world are less so than the chances of you getting struck by lightning.

Let's look at…

DANGERS OF TRAVELING

REAL VS FAKE

REAL DANGERS OF TRAVEL	FAKE DANGERS OF TRAVEL
Missing your bus	Being 'Taken'
Gaining Weight	Organs Harvested
Being overcharged	Finances hacked by Russians
Food poisoning	Bubonic Plague
Losing Sleep	Losing Sanity
Llama Attack	Terrorist Attack

I don't want to undermine anything. Yes, there are real dangers with travel. But 99.9% of traveller's worst case scenarios will involve something more along the lines of being ripped off by an aggressive salesman and less along the lines of being ripped apart by an aggressive bear.

So I want you to stop thinking about Hollywood movies. Stressing over being murdered in the woods (thanks 'Blair Witch'), kidnapped by Albanians (thanks 'Taken') or tortured mercilessly (thanks 'Hostel') is a complete waste of time and as we've already covered, time is precious.

I say **embrace** your fear.

It doesn't matter who you are or where you come from - your first international backpacking trip is going to scare the shit out of you. It's something new and something huge and something uncertain, and the combination of those three ingredients bakes a cake that would intimidate anyone.

What you have to understand that there is literally a small freaking army of people travelling the world independently at this very moment. I know it might be difficult to envision (especially if you've never been to a hostel) but you will be surrounded by other awesome people who are doing the exact same thing you are!

And the cool thing is that just like you, they had the same hesitations and fears!

So whatever your fears are, understand that they are a part of the process and they will evaporate pretty quickly once you are actually out there.

Being afraid is OK.

What is less OK is allowing that fear to shape your decisions, your experiences, and the opportunities in your life.

So don't do it – instead, acknowledge that fear and then step over it. After a few weeks on the road, you'll be like "HA!" I got this shit". You will become more confident, more assertive and more sure of your own abilities. Another point for team-travel.

Travelling to foreign countries might sound scary, but I vow to you, barring a one in a million tragedy, if you use your basic smarts you'll be fine. Being an independent traveler is not a path filled with danger and unless you are stupid (or stupid drunk) or point blank unlucky, you will be fine.

It's Not Always Easy

There are plenty of travel bloggers that paint travel as perfect. They describe travelling the world as an easy, sexy, glamorous event filled with beaches, spas and parties. Maybe it is like that for some people, but it certainly was never like that for me.

While travel is obviously the greatest invention since sliced bread - this description of travel is false advertising.

Let's be real.

Sometimes travel simply sucks.

Banking problems, aggressive salesmen, missed buses (always with the missed buses!), overbooked hostels, shitty food, getting sick, freezing my ass off, language barriers, dorm snorers, never ending humidity, seventeen hour airport layovers, I mean the list goes on and on, getting to the point that….

Sometimes travel SUCKS.

I don't want to discourage you from travelling. I'm just trying to paint a realistic picture and hit this on the head before continuing. I'll be sure to highlight shitty parts about travel (and most importantly, how to make them *less* shitty) as we go but I wanted to throw this out there now so you aren't expecting travel to be one none-stop glamorous event. Maybe for some people it can be but we're broke backpackers, it isn't like that for us and frankly travel without challenge, travel without difficulty, is just not as rewarding.

It's the same with anything in life. If you work for something, you appreciate it more. Some of the most unhappy people I have met have been people travelling the world in luxury, on family money. They've never worked a day in their life and they don't value money or experiences the same way that others do. They are looking for some intangible purpose.

They adopt and drop local religions, customs and fashions in an attempt to seem worldly. Sure, travelling with unlimited funds might look fun to the outside observer (and trust me, if somebody wanted to offer me a cocaine bikini model yacht party, I'd be down) but when you travel without challenge, you insulate yourself from the real world. You are an observer, not a participant.

So whilst travel can suck, that's part of the journey to. Life is always going to toss difficulties at you. The question is how well you dodge it. Travel is no exception. But would you rather rather deal with life's shit at home, or in a new and exciting location surrounded by new and exciting people? I know what I would pick...

Chapter Summary

At this point you should be excited.

But this, my friend, is just the beginning.

You've decided it's time. You are going to make the commitment to level up your travelling game. Let's take a look at what we discussed.

- *Everyone* wants to travel, and *anyone* can travel. The feeling is universal, and we are fortunate enough to live in a time where it's easier than ever.
- Travel is the ultimate opportunity
- Don't let family and friends hold you back. Yes, they mean the world to us, and it's difficult to shock them and let them down... but at the end of the day you need to do what's best for your life.
- You are going to die. Don't waste the best years of your life doing something you don't want to do. Our

time is finite, enjoy your life.

- Long term travel can be a great long term investment for your job and for your personal happiness. The lessons learned on the road will make you a stronger, happier person, and make you a more desirable candidate for hiring in competitive fields.

- Travelling independently can be scary... and that's OK. Remember that the difficulties of backpacking the world are part of the attraction – travel makes you stronger. This isn't a vacation - this is an opportunity to experience new things and find out what makes you tick.

Chapter Two
Travel Inspiration

So... What do you want out of travel?

It might seem like an odd question, but it's something I don't think enough people ask themselves.

You don't need to get super deep with your answer... just think about what you want. What do you envision happening?

When you're daydreaming about travelling, do you see yourself partying in a warehouse rave? Lounging on a deserted beach? Hiking through epic mountain ranges? Finding romance? Eating a certain type of crisp?

By identifying what you want out of travelling, you'll be able to get a good idea of which region of the world to start your adventure...

Why You Should Travel to Developing Nations

Aspiring travellers have a tendency to want to travel to certain parts of the world.

For instance, if this is your first epic backpacking trip... I have a sneaking suspicion you might be interested in going to...

1. Western Europe (if you're not from Western Europe)
2. Australia (If you're not from Australia)

3. USA/Canada (If you're not from the USA/Canada)

Am I wrong? Awesome! You win. Pass go and collect your $200.

But if I'm correct and you want to go to one of these three destinations - listen up.

Most aspiring travellers want to see these parts of the world. They dream of Parisian cafes, American road trips and the great Australian Outback.

And understandably so! Western Europe, Australia and the USA/Canada are freaking amazing. Each is a universe in itself. Each would take a lifetime and a half to properly explore, and even then you would only be scratching the surface.

But in my most honest of opinions, they are better avoided, *or at least limited to smaller doses.*

This is for two reasons.

1. These regions of the world aren't as culturally diverse as, say, India.

2. These regions of the world are damn expensive

And as much as I do want to place emphasis on the first point, the second is just as important.

Now, it is possible to travel to more expensive countries on a tight budget, the only problem is due to the high expenses your ability to have fun and live a little bit will be severely hampered. It's hard to have fun on $10 a day when a single beer costs 60% of your daily budget.

I've traveled extensively in developed countries. Believe it or not, I was able to travel to Japan, (one of the more expensive countries in the world to go backpacking) on $25 a day. It was an amazing experience, but I'll be honest - travelling in Japan on so small a budget was unbelievably difficult.

This is why you should towards developing nations. You

get a deeper cultural experience and more bang for your buck.

Would you prefer to A) travel to Japan on $25 a day and be in constant anxiety, roaming the streets in search of cheap food and lodging? Or B) travel to Venezuela on $10 a day and live like a king?

I hope you'll go with B.

Let's talk about where to go, and how each region of the world will vary. Once you understand what different parts of the world can offer, you can evaluate your personal wants and needs and be able to nail exactly where it is you want to go.

Should You Buy a Round the World Ticket?

Ahh, around the world itineraries. This is one of those things I legitimately forget that people actually do.

Around the world tickets are expensive, and while you often read about it on the internet, you don't really meet too many travellers on the road who are doing an 'around the world' tour.

That's because it's not quite all it's cracked up to be.

In my opinion, around the world plane tickets are overpriced, and a shitty compromise to what you *could* be doing. To me, the best way to travel is slowly… Take you time with your travels, and don't rush them.

Why You Shouldn't Do a Country in a Week

This is a real thing that real people do, and I need you to

understand why it sucks.

Pretentious traveler - "Yea I just got back from visiting ten countries"

Me - "Oh really, that's cool! Where?"

Pretentious traveler - "England, Scotland, France, Germany, Austria, Italy, Sweden, Hungary, Norway, and Iceland."

Me - "Cool! How long were you travelling for, that's a lot of ground!"

Pretentious Traveler - "Eight days."

Me - (Half astonished, half waiting for a punchline) "That's not even mathematically possible…"

Pretentious traveler - "Yea impressive I know, I'd probably say I was most impressed with the French cuisine, or should I say 'kee'zeen"

Me - How long were you in France for?

Pretentious traveler - "7 hours"

Me - "Answer this honestly….. Did you really visit Iceland or was that where your layover was?"

Pretentious traveler - "….You… don't count layovers?"

Unfortunately, showing off on the road, a travel story competition if you will, is all too common.

You see it all the time. Two travellers (usually sporting dreads) trying to out-do each other by any quantitative measure they can - country counts, languages spoken, cultures experienced, shit they climbed… You'll come across this at some point on your travels, sometimes it'll be from somebody with a bit of anxiety, trying to assert themselves. Sometimes, it'll be from someone who is just an asshole. Either way, these competitive boast-offs completely negate the entire point of travelling. It's not a competition. It's an experience, and going slowly is the best way to have that experience.

Not to say that travelling fast isn't fun. It's exhausting, but it can be a really great time!

But to me, fast travel cannot even begin to compare to slow travel. Blitzing through a country in less than a week is not the best way to travel. How deep into the culture can you really dive in five days? How much can you really learn?

Going to a country for a few days will be unavoidable, I've done it a few times but I really try to avoid it…

I've met people who were trying to visit an entire continent (South America) in just three weeks… All these guys are going to see are a ton of airports and frankly, I don't get the appeal.

For you, I highly recommend travelling slower. Get to know your new country. Establish some roots. Really learn to appreciate the food, language and overall culture for what it is! Don't travel fast to entertain yourself. *Get settled in the country you are in!* Only when you allow yourself to settle into a new country do you really start to understand new areas of the world.

Where to Start?

So, you get why you should travel slowly through developing nations, but where exactly should you start?

The answer is - go wherever you want!

This is not an over simplification, this is what travel is all about - serving yourself a delicious platter of whatever-the-hell-you-want!

But if you are unsure of what you want, let me help give you a bit of guidance…

My Favourite Backpacking Destinations

Well, in no particular order…

Myanmar is my favourite country in Southeast Asia and is packed to bursting with incredible treks, super friendly people, mysterious caves and the world's best temple ruins…

Iran boasts a fascinating history, beautiful women, stunning architecture, super easy hitchhiking and the most incredible hidden island in the world…

Venezuela is the cheapest country in the world where you can buy sixty beers for one dollar, climb the world's highest table-top mountain and fish for piranha in the jungle…

Nicaragua is one of the most fun countries I've ever been to and boasts incredible surfing, golden beaches, cheap cocaine and plenty of baby turtles…

Pakistan has the most beautiful landscapes I have ever seen, super friendly people and an emerging underground rave culture which is simply awesome…

The Philippines is cheap and packed to bursting with friendly, beautiful ladies and more isolated beaches and islands than you can possibly imagine…

The Places I Want to Go…

There are a lot of truly epic places in the world which I would love to explore, the best backpacking destinations on my wish list are…

Papua New Guinea boasts some of the world's most diverse rainforest and unexplored rivers plus dozens of un-contacted tribes. I hope to cross Papua New Guinea by kayak when I finally make it there!

Bhutan is famous for being the 'happiest country in the world' and is filled to bursting with absolutely insane treks and rarely visited monastery communities…

Yemen has been on my radar for ages, Socotra Island looks incredible…

Patagonia in Chile and Argentina is probably the most amazing place in the world to hire a campervan and go exploring…

New Zealand has been on my list since I was a kid! Unfortunately, it's the country that is the *furthest* from the UK and is pretty damn pricey to get to…

Types of Backpacking Trips

How do you want to travel the world? What do you want to get out of travel? I'll highlight varying regions of the world based on what they have in common.

Easy Peasy Backpacking Destinations

Great times and not a lot to worry about!
- Thailand
- The Philippines
- Turkey
- Train and hostel your way through Europe or Japan (if you've got the $$$)
- Nepal
- New Zealand

- South Africa
- Guatemala
- Greece

Cultural Backpacking Destinations

Plenty of culture and friendly locals!

- Iran
- Ghana
- Bolivia
- Georgia
- Ethiopia
- Mali
- Laos
- North Vietnam
- The Philippines

Religious Centre Backpacking Destinations

In search of inner peace...

- Rome
- Israel
- Nepal
- Tibet
- Myanmar
- Punjab or Varanasi in India
- Labella in the Ethiopian highlands

Overlanding Backpacking Adventures

Can be done by hitchhiking, public transport or your own vehicle…

- Istanbul – Cairo
- Cairo - Cape Town
- Mexico City – Panama City
- London – Hong Kong (via Trans Mongolian Railway)
- London – Istanbul
- London – Morocco
- London – Mongolia
- Bangkok – Bali
- Istanbul – Kathmandu

Beach Bum Backpacking Destinations

Build your very own sand-fortress…

- Mozambique
- Cuba
- Thailand
- The Philippines
- Australia
- South Africa
- Turkey
- Greece
- Goa in India
- Honduras
- Brazil
- Lagos in Portugal.

Great Introduction Backpacking Destinations

Safe and compact for those short on time…

- Guatemala
- Costa Rica
- Gambia
- Israel and Jordan
- Thailand and Cambodia
- New Zealand
- Goa in India
- Sri Lanka
- Uganda

Get High (in the Mountains)

Some of the world's best places to go trekking…

- Kyrgyzstan
- Tajikistan
- Chile
- Bolivia
- Nepal
- Tibet
- Kashmir and Ladakh in India
- Pakistan
- Afghanistan

Super Popular Backpacking Destinations

Okay so there may be plenty of other backpackers around but…

- Thailand, Laos, Cambodia, Vietnam, Malaysia and The Philippines

- Guatemala and Mexico
- Israel and Jordan
- South Africa
- Turkey, Greece and Egypt
- India, Nepal and Sri Lanka
- Brazil, Bolivia and Argentina
- New Zealand and Australia

Off The Beaten Path Backpacking Destinations

For those seeking 'real adventure'...
- Anywhere in the Middle East especially Yemen, Iraq, Afghanistan and Iran
- Myanmar (warning: get in while you can, this will change soon!)
- Papua New Guinea
- Ethiopia, Uganda, Ghana and Benin
- Mozambique, Cameroon and Zimbabwe
- Eastern European countries including Romania, Bulgaria, Serbia, Macedonia and Georgia
- Central Asian countries including Tajikistan, Mongolia and Kazakhstan
- North Korea
- Pakistan
- Andaman Islands in India
- Venezuela

Areas of Natural Beauty

Mountains, deserts, forests and icebergs...
- Pretty much all major mountain ranges, especially the

Alps and the Himalayas
- Stunning islands including Jamaica, Fraser Island in Oz and most of the Caribbean
- Antarctica
- Alaska
- The Caucasus
- The USA's national parks
- Great Barrier Reef in Australia
- Patagonia in South America
- Chile and the Bolivian Salt Flats
- Iguazu falls
- Galapagos islands
- Iceland
- Colombian coast
- Indonesia
- Amazon Rainforest
- Sahara desert in Morocco
- Lake Baikal in Russia
- Uluru rock in Australia

Epic Adventure Challenges

As opposed to picking a particular country or region, you could create a unique adventure. If you are particularly adventurous, or like the idea of a good challenge, there are a handful of epic itineraries that are sure to tickle your fancy.

Challenges can offer so much to your travels. A proper challenge gives your trip purpose. It gives you a clear itinerary - a beginning, middle and an end. Adventure challenges give you something specific to hone in on, and something tangible to accomplish. And believe me, the satisfaction upon completing such an itinerary is addictive. Before you know it, you'll be brimming with confidence and planning your next adventure.

Driving a Rickshaw across India

In 2016, my brother Alex and I embarked on our best bro-venture to date, we drove a beat-up old rickshaw, Tinkerbell, 2000 km across India.

It quickly became apparent that our rickshaw was beyond ancient and we had been hilariously ambitious in how much ground we hoped to cover in a day.

Driving a rickshaw 2,000 km across India over six weeks proved to be a totally nuts experience; it was, to my surprise, probably one of the toughest things I had ever attempted – mostly because we had to push-start the damn thing multiple times a day.

Over six weeks, Alex and myself developed a genuine love-hate bond with Tinkerbell. We got to know her wheezing, spluttering noises very well. I welded parts of her back together, tied important looking pieces to each other when they fell off in the middle of the road, I despaired, I wailed at her, I hugged her when she worked and cursed her when she didn't.

Our rickshaw race was an absolutely incredible bonding experience for myself and Alex and I ultimately fell in love with Tinkerbell.

We truly did get to see a side of India that I had never seen before; even after spending a year and a half backpacking in India. For a real adventure, you sometimes have to do something a little bit different.

Cycle the Silk Road

It sounds insane, and frankly it kind of is, but if you are the physically fit type and love to cycle, this is one of the most epic travel adventures you can do.

While there are a few varying routes, the beginning and end are the same, starting in East China and ending in Istanbul.

The most popular route includes cycling through the countries of China, Mongolia, Russia, Kazakhstan, Kyrgyzstan, Tajikistan, Uzbekistan, Turkmenistan, Iran, and finishing in Turkey.

13,000 kilometres and about 6 months of dedicated cycling. If you can pull this off, you can count yourself among the privileged few who can call themselves a 'real explorer'.

Patagonian Expedition Race

Teams of four go through deserted lands far from the influence of civilization. You'll trek, climb, swim, cycle and stumble across hundreds of kilometers in South Chile/Argentina.

This area is the very definition of isolated, as you'll be surrounded by some of the most gorgeous and untouched landscapes the world has to offer.

'Bagging' Peaks

Bagging is a slang term for hiking/mountain climbing enthusiasts. Bagging means setting a goal within a particular range of mountains.

A popular one is in the American Rockies. There are 53 peaks above 14,000 feet (4,200 kilometers). These mountains are known as *fourteen-ers*. To successfully *bag* the Rockies would be to successfully climb all 53 of these *fourteen-ers*.

Again, it's just a way to create a challenge by putting a hard number on the challenge.

But instead of the American Rockies, I recommend doing something similar, but in Pakistan.

The Himalayas are the tallest mountain range in the world. They dwarf the Rockies.

The Gilgit-Baltistan region of Pakistan has more than 100 peaks surpassing 20,000 feet (6,000+ meters). If you like to climb, you'll have your hands full with that!

Great Journeys of the World

A bit different from an *'adventure challenge'* - the great journeys of the world offer an epic itinerary. Less of a physical challenge, and more of a beginning, middle and end to truly see some amazing areas of the world.

- The Silk Road - Follow in the footsteps of Marco Polo and travel from West to East, soaking in incredible cultures as you journey through the 'Stans to China.
- UK to Bangkok - The recently opened India / Myanmar border means it is now possible to travel overland all the way from London to Bangkok. Consider hitchhiking across Europe and through Iran and Pakistan into India.
- Alaska to Tierra Del Fuego - One of the most ambitious journeys of all, start at the top of the world and end at the bottom; travelling from Alaska to the very tip of South America in Chile. I've read of many people cycling this trip (hint; it takes a long time).
- UK to Kathmandu - An oldie but a goodie, hippies first blazed this trail forty years ago. Hit the road and journey across Europe and onwards through Iran, Pakistan and India to the mighty Nepalese Himalayas.
- Mexico to Panama - A shorter Latino adventure for those with less time, spend three to six months, or even less if you're feeling fast, and travel from Mexico to Panama via Guatemala, Nicaragua, El Salvador, Honduras and Costa Rica.

- Brazil to Venezuela - Another crazy ambitious adventure, do a full loop of South America, starting in Brazil and ending in Venezuela.
- Interrailing Europe - A more expensive option but a great trip nonetheless, take on the whole of Europe by train.
- All around India - It's possible to spend a couple of years in India and only see about half of it, I should know. India offers a never ending, very budget friendly adventure and is packed with wildly different cultures, sights and peoples. Train travel around India is safe and cheap (highly recommended).
- South-East-Asia loop - The famed banana pancake trail is teeming with drunk eighteen year olds but hell, it's still fun. Travel through Thailand, Laos, Vietnam and Cambodia and extend the adventure with trips to Myanmar, The Philippines or Indonesia.
- Moscow to Beijing on Trans-Siberian - If you like vodka and endless stretches of wilderness, this could be the trip for you. Travel to China from Russia, pausing for some adventuring in Mongolia.
- Africa East Coast - Best attempted by motorbike or jeep, travel from Cairo to Cape Town taking in a dozen stunning African countries on the way.

Ultimately, the best way to start backpacking is to pick a region of the world and just go. It can be a part of the world you've wanted to travel through for years, or maybe a region that is just the beginning of an epic adventure challenge.

Regardless, picking a region as opposed to a few different countries around the world makes travelling cheaper, as you can go overland and travel slower (we'll come back to slow travel again later).

$10 A DAY
Best Countries in the World

SOUTHEAST ASIA

Cambodia, Laos, Malaysia, Myanmar, Thailand,
The Philippines, Vietnam

CENTRAL AMERICA

Guatemala, Honduras, Mexico*,
Nicaragua

SOUTH ASIA

Afghanistan, Bangladesh, India, Iran*,
Nepal, Pakistan, Sri Lanka

SOUTH AMERICA

Bolivia, Colombia, Guyana,
Paraguay, Peru, Venezuela

EASTERN EUROPE

Croatia, Estonia, Hungary, Latvia,
Macedonia, Poland, Romania, Russia,
Serbia, Slovakia, Ukraine, Czech Republic

www.TheBrokeBackpacker.com

I know, I know!

The list above is not completely accurate. For example, in the Central America section I included Mexico (it's in North America) and in South Asia I included Iran (which is in the Middle East).

Reason being while Mexico is not technically in Central America, it's next door neighbor to all of the countries mentioned, and you'd be crazy not to check out Mexico if you were in Central America, had you the chance.

Same thing with Iran. If you're in Pakistan, you better try and get your ass over there!

Eastern Europe has twenty-one countries, which would not all fit comfortably on the graphic, so I highlighted some of the best (and cheapest!).

South America has more countries than mentioned, but I highlighted the cheapest ones (it's damn difficult to do $10 a day in Brazil).

The infographic is loose, and is just meant to give you an idea of the areas that are broke backpacker friendly.

Which Region will you Choose?

I've highlighted the best areas in the world to travel. These regions are identified by the two most important factors - rich culture and low prices.

Look over the five options. Figure out which appeals to you most.

Here's some thoughts on each...

Central / South America

If you want to travel slowly, you can spend a lifetime in Central/South America. If you're on a budget, finding a ticket to another continent can be expensive, which is why if you want to check out this part of the world, I recommend doing so for a while.

One enormous pro to this area (aside from Latina women) is the language. Central and South America are linked by a unified language - Espanol!

Excluding Brazil (they speak Portuguese), Suriname (Dutch) and French Guiana (you guessed it, they speak French) the rest of the countries speak English and Spanish.

This is the only massive region of the world where such a luxury is available, and I want to emphasize just how awesome that is. After a year travelling Central/South America, you'll probably be very comfortable speaking in Spanish. Vamanos amigo!

Eastern Europe

Imagine the history, culture, architecture, and feel of Western Europe... But with half the tourists and a third of the cost.

Eastern Europe comes highly recommended, but it's honestly best to go in the summer.

Winter in many of these countries means sub zero temperatures, and maybe 2-3 hours of sunlight a day. I hitched and camped through Romania in the winter. Never again - it was excruciatingly cold.

A cool itinerary idea is to start in Eastern Europe, and as

the temperature drops, you can begin making your way overland to the Middle East through Turkey, and then into...

South Asia

I'm using this term a bit loosely as I want to cover Iran as well.

If I had to recommend one part of the world over another, it's probably South Asia.

Between India, Pakistan, Nepal and my (cheeky) inclusion of Iran, you simply cannot beat it.

It's a cultural orgasm mixed with some of the loveliest people and lowest prices you'll find in the world.

This is a part of the world that many people are afraid of. But after spending several years travelling extensively there, I can say it's one of the friendliest parts of the world.

Regardless, I do accept that the idea of backpacking this region of the world might intimidate certain people. I don't think it should! But I understand if it does. If you are looking for an easier introduction into the world of independent travel, I introduce thee to...

South East Asia

Ah yes. Good ol' S E of A. Most independent travellers have a special place in their heart for SE Asia, because most independent travellers probably started travelling there.

We've all eaten the crickets. Seen the temples. Drowned our livers in Thai buckets. It's hard to have a bad time in SE

Asia.

When it comes to ease of travel, Southeast Asia has got it figured out. SE Asia might still be the easiest in terms of overall infrastructure. You don't really have to work for anything in SE Asia, it's so well travelled - the hostels and locals have backpackers figured out.

But while the convenience is nice, it's reputation makes it significantly more saturated, and getting truly off the beaten track requires a bit more effort. Another disadvantage is that the cost of backpacking in South East Asia is no longer as low as it used to be.

Frankly though, South East Asia is awesome. Thailand and Cambodia may have lost a bit of their charm as more and more tourists visit but Myanmar and The Philippines still offer plenty of real adventures. From a socialising point of view, it's hard to beat SEA, the parties in Laos and Thailand are legendary. However, if you want to stretch your money a bit further, and aren't as interested in the mad-party-drinking scene then you might want to start somewhere else.

So Where Should You Go!?

It used to be that SE Asia was the spot to start - it used to be a sort of rite of passage. And there's still an argument to be made that it is, but the independent travel scene has picked up significantly around the world, and any one of these regions will cater to a newbie traveler.

If you are a newbie and looking for somewhere to go, pick one of these five.

And here's my next bit of advice.

If you want to do an around the world trip, go for it! But wait until you are in your region of choice to make any next-step decisions.

For example, if you pick Eastern Europe, dive into Eastern Europe. Go balls to the wall! But every now and then keep an eye on Skyscanner. Amazingly cheap fares pop up all the time. After a few months of travelling around the Slavic side of the world on $10 a day, you might find a cheap flight to India, Morocco, or Thailand!

Random examples, but if you really want to experience the best that travel has to offer, you'll be willing to go with the flow. I'll touch up a bit more on this later as well.

Chapter Summary

- Figuring out where to start can be tough, so the best way is to identify what it is you want from travel. Beaches? Mountains? Parties? Culture? History? Figure out what it is you want to see. By doing so you'll be able to figure out where to begin.
- Consider an adventure or specific itinerary. Doing so puts an amazing new angle on your travels as you now have a tangible goal. If you complete the goal you'll feel amazing, and if plans change and you go rogue - so be it!
- Limit your time in the Big Three (Western Europe, North America, Australia) and place an emphasis on developing countries. Doing so will expose you to more interesting cultures and places, but you'll also spend a fraction of the money.

- Be ready to travel slowly. Don't be that guy who tries to see India in four days or South East Asia in two weeks. Travel long, travel slow. Doing so will enable you to dive deeper into the culture and save more money.

- Pick a region and GO FOR IT! Don't over think it. If you're not sure where to go then grab a dart and throw it at a map… I've selected destinations this way in the past. Once you have your spot, buy the ticket and go. Don't put off your adventure, it's waiting for you.

Chapter Three
Travel Planning

(A.K.A Winging it like a Boss)

Do you want to know my secret to happy long term travels?

It involves a plan.

The best kind of plan.

No plan.

Well, OK, not exactly no plan but more the ability to travel without losing yourself in endless planning.

Travel is like life. You might have plans for life. But life will have other plans for you.

The quicker you learn to give up control while travelling (specifically referring to *the need to plan*) the quicker you'll be able to slow down and soak in the experience. Planning has its place since visas, flights and other bits and pieces do sometimes need to be worked out in advance but it's crucial that you stay chill and learn to be flexible.

Why You Should Stay Flexible

Being flexible is very important as it can improve your posture as well as improve the function of muscles and joints.

Different kind of flexible.

Flexibility when travelling won't improve your posture, but it will likely improve your experience!

When you are travelling, you are going to meet some of the coolest people you have ever met in your entire life.

And the people you meet on your travels might impact your life in small ways.

But often, the people you meet in your travels will impact your life in **enormous** ways. You'll get high in the mountains together, throw paint at each other in Nepal, fall in love and maybe even save each other from a knife wielding Indian man (all things that have happened to me).

I can't even begin to tell you how many amazing people I've met on my travels, and how my encountering them completely changed my entire plan.

And it makes sense when you think about it, doesn't it?

Example time. You spent a few weeks visiting a friend in Hong Kong, and while you were there, you bought a flight to Vietnam, and two weeks after that a flight to Thailand, and a week after that a flight to Australia.

Hong Kong -> Vietnam -> Thailand -> Australia. Sounds dope right?

But you get to Ho Chi Minh, check into your hostel, and make a few new friends. Then after a few days you and these quick friends become close friends. Before you know it, you're engaged in a passionate fling with one of your new amigos. Your friends are going to buy motorcycles, and drive up to Northern Vietnam over the course of a month. Once they get there they plan to sell the bikes to make their money back, then head into Laos for an epic month on the Nam Song River.

Um. Yes. Count me in!

Except now you have to make a choice. You see, you

decided to plan ahead... a bit *too far* ahead. Your money is invested in three flights getting you to Australia. But your heart is now invested with your new friends and getting to Laos by motorcycle.

What do you do?

What you do is take mental note of this sad hypothetical story and make sure to remember - flexibility is the name of the game!

Why Your Plans Will Change

You will meet a lot of amazing people on the road. You will bond with each other, you will connect with each other, you will change each other's lives.

And this my friends, is what travel is really all about.

Yes, it's the new countries, and the cultures and food and threesomes in bunk-beds. But the everlasting memories will be of the people you met, and how they inevitably ended up changing your plans, and they changed yours.

They changed mine (cue personal story).

In January 2016, I hitchhiked up Turkey and into Georgia. I spent my birthday wasted with a bunch of friendly Georgians on cheap vodka and, with a hell of a headache, hit the road a few days later and pushed on to Iran.

This was a dream of mine! I had always wanted to go to Iran. It's a country that had fascinated me for years and after a lot of back and forth I finally managed to get myself an Irish passport (at the time Brits could only enter Iran on an organised tour).

Finally Iran was open to me. I hitched to Tehran and

began to plan my next moves; I had a month on my visa and needed to cover some serious ground to make it to Pakistan.

Remember I said how everything can change? In my story, a day later - everything changed.

I met a girl for a coffee and we spent ten hours chatting, the day flew by, turning to night. The next week tumbled by madly as I hitchhiked to Kurdistan. I hit deep snow and my planned hikes became impossible, so I turned around and headed back towards the girl in the coffee shop.

I met her in a small town and we fell into a passionate relationship. I asked her if she wanted to hitchhike around Iran with me and a couple of days later, to get around Iran's strict laws regarding foreigners mixing with local women, we got a temporary Islamic marriage.

Fast forward a year and Esme and I are heading into the Bhutanese mountains on another adventure.

And this is just one example of how travelling the world can change your life, can present you with the most unexpected of opportunities and the most unlikely of friendships.

Choosing the Best Time to Travel

Ok, enough with the sappy stuff. Let's do what all human beings do when there's a void in conversation. Talk about the weather.

Actually, travel and climate do have a very interesting relationship. If you notice every major tourist destination has a high season and a low season.

Western Europe? High season in summer. Low season in winter.

South East Asia? High season in winter. Low season in summer.

Some high seasons are a big chunk of the year. Some high seasons are a very small window of the year.

What dictates high and low season?

The weather.

Frankly, high season will usually have lovely weather, and low season will usually have not-as-lovely weather.

This isn't an end all for high/low season. I've experienced some fantastic weather in low season in Pakistan, and by no means is high season a guarantee that the skies will be clear and blue.

So with this information, high season makes sense! Everything is paradise! Think 22 Celsius (72 Fahrenheit) with blue skies. This is Thai beaches in January, Barcelona in July, Rio in December and Siberia... never.

But with this beautiful weather comes an influx of beautiful (and not so beautiful) tourists.

High season is lovely, but wherever you are, you need to understand that you won't have it to yourself.

LOW SEASON VS HIGH SEASON

THE CASE FOR LOW SEASON

LOW SEASON	HIGH SEASON
Elbow room!	Suffocated by people
Half the price	Three times the price
More authentic	A show for tourists
Can barter more	Can barter less

In general, the only disadvantage of travelling in low season is that the weather might be more challenging. So if you're someone who doesn't mind intense heat or cold… consider travelling to places in low season.

Often, but not always, when you do travel to a country in low season you will discover that the weather really isn't that big of a problem and hell – you are the only person there.

I visited Pakistan and Nepal in the months of January and February and felt like I had the country to myself. High season is September to November, so by waiting a few months, I experienced a completely different Nepal and Pakistan to what many backpackers see. It was truly amazing to be in such a special place and to have it all to myself.

And while the weather was certainly colder (10 degrees Celsius average), it was still good trekking weather.

This is why low season rocks. You get cheaper prices, less annoying tourists and a much more authentic experience.

Saying that, you must avoid some countries during certain times of the year – I do not recommend travelling in India or Myanmar during the monsoon season, it'll be damn hot. In general, you don't need to worry about the weather too much but do spend five minutes googling before you book your flights so you have a rough idea of what to expect when you get out there. Often, the best time to visit any destination is just before or just after high season.

Most Travel Guides Are Bullshit

That's right! I said it. Most travel guides aren't worth buying. Here's why...

1. They become outdated very quickly. A travel blogger can update his 'Uruguay Travel Guide' with a few clicks of a mouse. If Lonely Planet wants to update a travel guide they have to update and reprint an entire publication – something they are happy to do because it means they can make even more money.

2. Companies like Lonely Planet and Frommers focus way too much on hotel and inn reviews (because they are frequently bribed to do so).

3. Most travel guides are writing for baby boomers and people more interested in travelling like a tourist. Independent travelers choose to experience the world in a different way... partly because we are broke.

4. Lonely Planet actively condemns hitchhiking. These guys never camp, they never couchsurf, they never do any of the stuff that makes travel accessible and affordable to the unwashed masses (that's you, and me). They are completely out of touch with today's generation of broke backpackers.

5. Because of all these points, travel bloggers tend to have better researched, more up-to-date, closer to the ground, information. I never buy a guidebook but I will take to the internet if I need to research a destination I want to travel to.

Travel Blogs

So if you need information about a destination pre-arrival, and travel guides are not reliable, what are you supposed to do?

Cue: travel blogs. They're not all perfect, but a handful are pretty good.

Instead of recommending *specific* travel bloggers, I'm going to recommend a strategy for finding great information *from* travel bloggers. Because let's be honest, there's thousands of travel bloggers, and not all of them are in it to win it.

The same problems I have with guidebooks can also be an issue with travel blogs! My strategy is pretty simple - find the most recent information.

Google search in all of its glory doesn't always work well with travel guides. Often the results at the top have been there for a while, and while they may have been up to date when written, they're likely out of date now.

So simply - take a stroll through Google. If you're heading to Jamaica, search for *Jamaica Backpacker Guide* or *Jamaica Travel Guide,* or *Backpacking Jamaica.* Then scroll through the results to find something recently published.

The final test is to make sure the tone of the article is down to earth. If the article starts off talking about how great the luxury beach resort was… move on to the next.

Once you find a site with a recently published article and a tone you can relate to - run with it!

Handy Apps

For a long time, I travelled the world without a phone or laptop. It was a simpler, and in some ways, better time. These days, I travel with both a phone and laptop but I make a concerted effort to limit my time on both. The thing is, if you're stuck on your phone, putting up an invisible barrier between you and people around you, you are less likely to have a random encounter.

Random encounters are one of the best parts of travelling; making friends with a local and ending up on a night out at a jazz bar where you meet a sexy lady and dance the night away…

Seriously though, being on your phone can hamper you from properly exploring a country and whilst technology does make everything easier, it also makes you less adept at solving real problems.

Having said that, there's a few apps in particular that makes travelling less of a headache. Here's a few of my favourites…

Maps.me

Maps.me is free, easy to use, and most importantly you can use the maps offline with turn by turn navigation. This is a must have if you are travelling through somewhere like Pakistan or Iran.

XE

Some currency conversions are easy.

1 Euro is usually around 1 Dollar. Got it!

Some currency conversions are difficult.

1 British Pound is 28185.72 Vietnamese Dongs. What the heck?

I introduce thee to XE.

Currencies can be tough, especially when hopping around countries. XE makes it easy. It also works offline.

Skype and Instant Messaging Services

Viber, Whatsapp, Telegram, Facebook Messenger – there are a lot of different instant messaging services out there which allow you to stay in touch with people and send photos, voice messages and even your location.

Different people from different parts of the world use different platforms. If you meet someone from Ukraine, they're probably going to use Viber. If you meet someone from Japan, they're probably going to use Line. China is dominated by WeChat. Iranians all use Telegram.

While there are a handful of options, the most popular are Whatsapp and Facebook messenger.

Download those before you go and download the others if needed on the road.

Finding a Flight Online

For flights I'll typically use a combination of Skyscanner and Secret Flying.

Skyscanner is a flight search engine and is hand's down the best one I've come across for finding dirt cheap flights plus it's pretty easy to use.

A lesser known resource is Secret Flying.

Secret Flying capitalizes on 'mistake fares' or extremely cheap fares. It isn't quite a search tool, but something to keep an eye on and check periodically. I've written an entire post on how to find the cheapest flights, go check it out on the blog. Take a peek at the last few pages of the book for a full list of all of the online resources I use to plan my adventures.

The Backpacker Grapevine

No other resource will hold a candle to the value of the backpacker grapevine.

What is the backpacker grapevine?

After a long day of travelling, walking, and seeing cool sights, the sun starts to set and many a backpacker wants to sit down and drink five or six beers whilst chatting to their fellow travelers.

The backpacker grapevine is just a fancy name for backpackers telling each other where they've been and seen, and it's best done over a beer… or a gin and tonic if you're watching your abs.

"Oh you're going to Iran? We were there just

there last week, epic place!"

"I know people don't speak highly of it, but I thought Phnom Penh was actually pretty cool!"

"You're going to the waterfall? I went yesterday. Some dude I met here a few days ago said the bus ride was terrible, so we took a cab and split it three ways, it was only a few bucks each"

"Ok I know that it's a bit expensive, but I did this food tour yesterday, and it was the best experience I've had in Indonesia yet. I think you should check it out"

"But listen to me, when you rent the surfboard make sure to check it's sturdy! The instructors don't tell you this but if it breaks, you gotta pay for it. Happened to some guy I met in Playa Gigante last week"

"Yea, Hagia Sophia was cool, but not really worth the entrance fee."

"Whatever you do dude, you HAVE to check out Cenote Dos Ojos, no one was there and the water was perfect!"

"Don't buy the shots at Glow, we did but they were definitely watered down"

"Actually the hike really wasn't as tough as I thought it was going to be, but I definitely recommend bringing your own water. There were no shops until the very end of the trail, and it was expensive."

"The hostel bartender sells weed"

"Hitching wasn't easy, a lot harder than it was in Poland. I'd say it took us a good two hours before we were able to get our first ride"

The backpacker grapevine. It's kind of like backpacker gossip, but in time you will find it is far more reliable than any guidebook, app or website you'll ever find. It's real, up to date information, from a real, up to date person who isn't pushing any alternative agenda.

Long live the backpacker grapevine.

Dealing with Visas

If there was ONE thing that gets in the way of the carefree, flexible traveler, it's freaking visas!

Visas can get sticky and messy, and differ from country to country, and nationality to nationality.

My advice? Visa as you need. (And yes, I just used the word *'visa'* as a verb.)

Given the impulsive behavior of travellers and the high cost of visas, getting any visas without being certain you are entering the country is not recommended.

Get what you need, when you need it.

Having said that, if you are driven to go somewhere that requires a visa, you'll need to get it beforehand and do a little planning (like me going to Iran).

Sometimes you'll be able to pick up visas on arrival or at an embassy in an adjacent country…. But it's not always the case.

Certain countries (particularly in the Middle East and Asia) will require a lot of time and effort to obtain a visa. Visa processes for Pakistan, India, Iran, Brazil, China, Russia can be very challenging depending on your nationality.

Making a Decision about Getting Stressed

Visas. Lodging. Money. Flights. Currency exchange. Messaging apps. Is your head spinning yet?

Before we continue I want to emphasize something.

In life, we have plans, we prepare ourselves to the best of our ability, and think we are ready to handle whatever life throws at us.

Then shit hits the fan, and everything gets turned upside down.

Travel is no different. You might have visas lined up, plane tickets purchased and have all your ducks in a row…But I promise you, stuff will go wrong.

The important thing is realizing that early on and promising yourself that when mishaps occur, you won't let it ruin your trip.

I mean, think of it this way, if you are expecting that things will go wrong - what's the point of stressing?!? You knew it was coming! You didn't know exactly *what* was going to go wrong, but you prepared yourself for the fact that something *would* go wrong.

So what's the point of stressing?

Stress is a choice, and a bad one. It builds anxiety which manifests itself physically in awful ways.

Choose not to get stressed. Don't sweat the small stuff, and while you're at it, try not to sweat the big stuff either.

Chapter Summary

- Flexibility is the name of the game. Try your best to let go of your need for control. You'll realize the happiest travellers are the ones who let life happen and simply choose to go with the flow. Because...

- Your plans will change! You are going to be in new places, meeting new people and experiencing new things. You might think you want to go somewhere new, but you never really know until you're there.

- High season and low season each have their pros and cons. Honestly, the weather in low season is rarely as bad as it's made out to be and can leave you saving a lot of money and having to deal with less tourists. But if you can swing it - aim for just before or just after high season.

- Travel guides are mostly bullshit. They write for baby boomers and people on weekend holidays. Their advice doesn't cater to the kind of travel you want to do. The best way to get some research in is by looking for up to date information on blogs you trust because you can...

- Trust the backpacker grapevine! Blogs and guidebooks can be alright, but at the end of the day you are going to end up trusting people you meet on the road. A personal opinion goes a lot further than some random blogger's opinion.

- Don't go app crazy, but download the few essentials. Whatsapp, some currency app, and some maps app will be all that you really need. And even then, don't completely rely on them!

- Only get the visas you need to get. This can be a challenge as you might think you want to go somewhere, but I only recommend getting the visa if you are 100% certain. Then once you get the visa, you can figure out your plans from there.
- Fuck stress.

Chapter Four
Finances

Money.

God damn money.

It's the root of all evil, but there's no real way to get around it is there? Although, Bitcoin is doing it's damn best...

Unfortunately, money issues are something every good traveler (bitterly) accepts. Money sucks, but if you want to travel, you need to accept that you must know it's ways and most importantly, you need to learn how to spend *less* of it.

I spent years mastering the art of budget travel. I failed often. When I started there wasn't anywhere near the amount of information or resources that are available now.

Lucky for you, my nine years of global travel has sharpened my skills, and I am ready to share all of my financial strategies.

How Much Money Do You Really Need?

This depends. Remember earlier on when we talked about your travel expectations? This is where money comes into play.

If you envision yourself at trendy clubs in Ibiza, or sipping $20 cocktails on skyscraper rooftop pools in Singapore, I will tell you right now, you're going to need a ton of money.

But hopefully if you've gotten this far, you realize that that kind of travel doesn't compare to a more immersive, longer experience. The amount of money you could spend in five days in Ibiza could last you three months travelling in India or Central America.

I want to teach you how to travel the world perpetually. If that sounds more like your cup of tea, you can do it with very little and sometimes even zero money in the bank.

How do I know this?

Because I travelled the world for years with absolutely no money in the bank.

Hence, the **Broke** Backpacker.

When I travelled, I did so broke AF.

And yet I still made it all over the globe.

Money is only as big a hurdle as you let it be, if you truly want to live a life of adventure; you will find a way to overcome your lack of money, usually that means sacrificing comfort – it's a sacrifice that is well worth the reward.

Saving Up Money

Different people will different reactions to the concept of travelling broke. While it works for me, you might be uncomfortable with the idea.

But while the thought might make you a bit uncomfortable… you'll learn so much from travelling with no money.

Have you ever heard the saying *"what doesn't kill you makes you stronger"?* I think this perfectly embodies what travelling broke is all about.

Travelling the world on $10 a day will give you experiences that other travellers only dreamed of, and because of those experiences, it will build character in ways you never thought possible.

Having said that, there are two distinct cases where I recommend saving up money for travelling.

1. You're the type of person who has to have a safety net
2. You can't travel right away, so you might as well put some money in the bank!

The first point is easy. If the thought of travelling with no money makes your skin crawl, then OK, no worries, we are all different. The important thing is that you've decided to travel, and travel you shall!

Having money is awesome because it offers you peace of mind. If your nerves are tingling with the thought of travelling the world, then maybe a few dollars in the bank will help take the edge off.

Not everyone can hit the road right now and whilst I do think it's important to draw a line, to set a date on when you will start your adventure, I understand that sometimes there are commitments which it makes sense to see out.

Maybe you've got another semester at Uni. Perhaps your brother's wedding is in a few weeks. Potentially, you have a couple of months of rent already paid for.

Whatever the reasons may be, if you can't start your backpacking life tomorrow, the best thing you can do is start saving some cash up for when you do hit the road.

If this sounds like you, do yourself a favor - pick a number, cut it by 25%, **and stick with it.**

If you don't pick a hard number, the need to save money will constantly be an excuse. It will become an ever evolving obstacle that will only serve as a deterrence for your travels. And then, you'll face a difficult decision – you will end up with enough money to put a deposit on a house and you will have to choose between travelling and 'the logical step'.

Pick a number. Reach your goal. Get out and see the world. Don't let an evolving financial quota become another excuse to delay your dreams.

Money Saving Tips

What are some money making tactics while you're counting down to your launch into the world?

My recommendation? Go Japanese!

The Japanese culture is unique in the world for their fascinating obsession with minimalism. It is one of the few cultures on the planet to have a *'less is more'* attitude. Their homes, their possessions, their decorations - everything!

So I repeat, go Japanese, and minimalize your life.

First off, you'll need to lower your expenses.

Sell your car. Start taking the bus. Cut down on the $4 Starbucks coffees and start brewing your own. Whatever you do, cut it out of your life, or figure out a way to continue doing it at a fraction of the price.

If you like to drink out at night, spend 90% less, buy a six pack and drink at home.

If you like to go out on dates, do it at coffee shops over tea instead of the trendy new Latin American restaurant with $20 appetizers.

If you like to work out, cut the $50 a month gym membership and start an at home routine.

Anything you are spending money on can be done at a fraction of the price.

And to make a bit extra money...

Get rid of your stuff. Don't throw it away - sell it! Sell all of it.

Who cares if it's only seventy bucks extra. Seventy bucks could get you an extra week in India. Totally worth the effort.

You can also look online for freelancing gigs or pick up a second job.

This is the way I look at it.

Let's say you give yourself three months to save every last penny you possibly can.

Sure, maybe that three months is just plain out boring. You're home. You're saving money. But you're bored.

Do yourself a favor, and consider that while these mere ninety days might be monotonous and dragging out... by doing this you are going to be able to be on the road for **nine months**.

It's a small price to pay for a way to launch yourself into freedom. Plus the challenge will be a good test of your ability to spend less and gauge your overall personal discipline.

I know you want to date. I know you want to drink. I know you want to have fun.

And you will.

Because you are going to do all of those things while on the road.

So do yourself a favor. If you have to save some money - pick a number, and be done with it as fast as possible. You'll thank yourself.

Making Money While Travelling

As my Spanish amigos would say - this information is *muy importante!*

Unless you have a large amount of money squirreled away, you will eventually need to figure out a way to earn some money on the road or your travels will come to an abrupt end when you can no longer afford your visas.

There are basically two ways to make money while travelling.

1. With a laptop
2. With your hands

The most lucrative ways to make money whilst travelling is by starting your own career as a digital nomad.

But sometimes, backpackers need to make money (or save money) quickly and earning money online is a slow burn. If you need to earn money quickly, there are plenty of options...

Finding Work on The Road

If you are looking for work while travelling, there are two strategies.

1. Find something more permanent and plant yourself in a new place for a while
2. Find something quick and easy to make a couple extra bucks

When I think of option #1 (planting yourself somewhere) the first thing that comes to mind is teaching English. It's an extremely proven way to make money and see the world.

Another way to follow the first strategy is to accept a long term WWOOFing gig, or an Au-Pair contract.

The second option usually involves quick work for low pay, but pay nonetheless! This is more along the lines of finding some quick work in a bar or hostel, or anything else that pays room and/or cash.

So I put together a list of the best travel jobs for backpackers whilst on the road. These are the jobs that allow you to work and travel the world without having to worry about running out of cash...

Best Travel Jobs

Teach English abroad

You can teach English in so many countries these days and see the world at the same time. You can give yourself even more freedom by teaching English online and it's possible to score some very high paying gigs if you have good hustle.

Being a native speaker gives you an obvious advantage but it's also possible for non-native speakers to get work teaching English too. Taking a TEFL course first will help you hit the ground running and hopefully will mean you won't be a crap teacher. It's a small investment that will help you get a better paying job.

Scuba instructor

Being a certified Scuba Diver Instructor takes a bit of investment, but can be one of the most fun ways to work and travel. You need a handful of courses and certifications, as well as having logged in a certain amount of hours underwater yourself. If you are already certified, get excited! If you aren't, you can do it at home, or take advantage of many programs that exist in countries like Thailand and The Philippines. It's a seriously well paying travel job!

Surfing instructor

Surfing instructors can do well for themselves by travelling, surfing, meeting people who are interested and want to learn, and then offering their services. It won't be as well paying as scuba instruction, but you'll be getting paid to do surf work and travel which is probably the coolest thing ever.

Teach yoga

Yoga has emerged in popularity around the world, and Yoga instructors are in high demand. While not the highest paying job, finding work as a Yoga instructor is one of the more assured ways to work and travel. Getting certified certainly helps you stand out from the crowd, but isn't needed. Talk to other guests at your hostel, or even better, throw up some courses on Udemy or similar online education sites.

Buy a place and rent it

If you have been working for a while, you may have some savings. Rather than blowing it all on a couple of fast paced years of travel, invest it into buying a property at home and renting it out whilst you travel (living off the rent money). You can advertise your place on lots of different websites including Airbnb. It can easily turn into big bucks: so much so that some of my friends will not even stay at their own place when they return to their hometown. They'll keep renting it out and stay somewhere else.

Work on a boat

Unfortunately, the days of being a pirate are kinda over but that doesn't mean you can't still be a modern day 'kind-of pirate'. Still a bit under the radar, it's very possible to find travel jobs on boats, specifically - yachts and sailboats. Work is certainly easier to get with experience, but sometimes it's as easy as just walking onto a dock and asking around. If you are interested in working and travelling on yachts or sailboats, check out www.findacrew.net.

Work on a cruise ship

Cruise ships are one of the best travel jobs out there - you just gotta be ready to **work**! Cruise ships span the globe and work is easily found. It's a work-hard play-hard atmosphere. You'll be doing 60 hour weeks of work, and partying at nights and exploring ports with your co-workers. One phenomenal perk to working on a cruise ship is the ability to save money. The jobs usually only pay $1,000-$2,000 a month, but with no car, no bills, no insurance, no **nothing** to pay for, it all goes straight into your savings account (or, if you're smart, you'll put it in Bitcoin). Cruise ships are a great way to work hard, see the world, and finish your contract with a *boatload* of money saved up.

Boat delivery

A bit difficult to get into as a newbie, but if you have some experience on the high seas, boat delivery has some serious work and travel potential. Typically the pay won't be very high (if at all) but you'll get your experience up and get to sail the seven seas for free! Getting into this line of work could lead to more lucrative gigs in the future. Check out www.crewseekers.com or www.cruisersforum.com for some job leads!

WWOOFing

WWOOFing (World Wide Opportunities on Organic Farms) has been budget travellers go-to for decades now. The gist is - you work on organic a farm for 20-30 hours a week and are given free food and accommodation in return. There are tens of thousands of farms spanning the globe, so wherever you wish to travel, WWOOF's got you!

HelpX

Similar to WWOOFing, HelpX has been around for a while. You haven't earned your budget travel stripes until you've HelpX-ed somewhere! HelpX, and Workaway (next on the list) are very similar. As opposed to WWOOFing (which is volunteer work exclusively on farms) these two sites have a range of volunteering tasks. Teaching English, translating, painting, hostel work, watching kids, farming - anything!

Workaway

Similar to HelpX, Workaway allows you to volunteer for free food and lodging. Workaway is a bit newer than HelpX, but has grown in popularity very quickly, becoming the preferred out of the two for many travellers.

Housesitting

Sort of a work-exchange-meets-a-job, House Sitting is all the hype right now. Typically you pet-sit for an extended amount of time, and in return are given free reign over an entire house! Housesitting gigs rarely pay, but you can't really complain. You'll be getting free accommodation, a big ass kitchen, and the privacy of your own house! This is one of the best ways to travel. As with all good things, it's challenging to crack into, but once you gain experience and a resume, you'll have your choice of gigs. Highly recommended!

Work as an Au Pair

Au-Pairing is one of the oldest travel jobs around and is still a great option to save some money and see the world. Personally, kids ain't for me. However, if you are bubbly, happy, smiley and don't mind clearing up sick then there's plenty of little ones who need a lovely person like *you* to help take care of them. It doesn't always pay, and if it does pay it's not always much but you can earn up to 5k a month if you're happy to teach in some more far-flung lands like Saudi Arabia. You'll get free lodging and food, and likely some pocket change for the weekend if you're volunteering in Europe.

Translation work

If you have a knack for learning other languages quickly, you should consider becoming a translator and working online or offline to fund your travels. I have zero experience with this as I am relatively talentless when it comes to languages.

Hostel work

Hostel work is one of those unspoken backpacker rules. It's on the web a bit, but it's still pretty hush hush. So let me tell you - finding hostel work is usually very simple. One of the easiest travel jobs to get - just ask the hostels you are staying at if they are looking for any help. They will know exactly what this means. "Help" means working the front desk graveyard shift, sweeping the floors, or most likely minding the bar. We'll cover this a bit more in a bit.

Bar work

Similar to hostel work, bar work has kept the backpacker going since basically the dawn of time. Often the bar work will be in a hostel bar (mentioned above) but just as legit is finding work at standalone bars. This is particularly true in seasonal European cities (but I've seen it in South America, Australia, Asia - basically everywhere). The best way to find work is just to walk around and ask if the bars are looking for any help, or if you're having a pint somewhere, strike up a conversation with the bartender and get the scoop. A simple inquisition can lead to a lot of opportunities.

Seasonal jobs

This is a large category that encompasses many different jobs. Restaurants, construction, hotels, cruise ships, fishing boats, ski resorts, the list goes on! While a lot of these jobs are covered elsewhere in this post, seasonal jobs are worth noting. You can literally travel the world, chasing season (which by the way usually equates to amazingly beautiful weather) and making money when jobs are in demand and at their highest paying.

Construction

One can find legitimate and decent paying construction work in Australia or New Zealand. In other parts of the world, asking around can bring also bring a lot of opportunities. If you have construction experience heed my advice - check out WWOOF, HelpX and Workaway. Many hostels, farms, and everything in between will advertise their needs in hopes of finding a qualified traveler. You'll get food, lodging, and (depending on the project) a bit of money as well.

Become a freelance photographer

If you love taking pictures and you are good at it, why aren't you making the most of your skills and being paid for it? Breaking into freelance photography is no easy feat but it is totally possible if you have perseverance and work at honing your craft every day.

Tour director

A Tour Director accompanies a tour group for the entirety of the itinerary and basically makes sure people are having a good time. If it's a twenty one day culture tour through Central America, the Tour Director is there the entire time, leading the group, answering questions, communicating with the bus driver, and most importantly creating solutions when shit goes wrong.

This is one of the travel jobs that requires the most work, but if you think you possess the qualities, there are thousands of tour operations companies looking for new leaders.

Travel tour guide

As opposed to a Tour Director, a Tour Guide usually does shorter tours (think three-hour walking tours). Ideally, Tour Guides are experts in their niche, but sometimes a bit more knowledge than the average Joe will suffice. If you have experience or certification, getting tour guide work will be easy.

If you live within the EU, you can also find tour guide work within Europe relatively easy (Free Walking tours, etc.) without certification. Otherwise, there are lots of people on the web tapping into their entrepreneurial spirit and starting their own tours while on the road.

Fitness instructor

Similar to Yoga, if you're in shape and know how to break a sweat, you can get paid to help others do the same! I love finding creative ways to stay in shape while travelling, and you'll find plenty of other travellers who will share this interest. See if your hostel wants to organise any activities or events which you can market by word of mouth off by putting a flyer up. Head to a park or the beach and BOOM! You're a certified fitness instructor... sort of. We'll touch up on fitness while on the road a bit further down the line.

Physio therapy / Masseuse

If you are a physio therapist or a fully trained masseuse, you can make bank by advertising your services in hostels – I have met a couple of people travelling the world this way.

Professional chef

If you have experience working in a restaurant, then you'll know that it's a very transient industry. Employees come and go in short spurts, only to be replaced by others, who then do the exact same thing. It's just the way the industry works. But this benefits the traveler! If you have some cooking abilities or some legitimate kitchen experience you can find work by asking around at kitchens in hotels, cruise ships, boats, or retreats. Also take a look into WWOOF, HelpX and Workaway as you can certainly find some cook-work opportunities for a free place to stay.

Making and selling jewellery

Screw travel jobs, be a travel entrepreneur! While you can make and sell anything, Jewellery is certainly the backpacker artisans staple and I've met lots of people who make and sell jewellery whilst travelling.

Think about it. The materials can be cheap and light to carry, it's an artsy/fun thing to do, and you can set up shop (busking style) in a city and make some money! Selling handmade jewellery on the street isn't the path to becoming a billionaire, but if you can make a decent product, it's a great way to bring in enough to cover a day of gallivanting. You can also sell your jewellery online using Etsy, eBay, or Instagram.

Personal imports

A personal favourite of mine, this is what I sometimes refer to as the *'stuff your backpack'* method. When in exotic countries you will find awesome knicks and knacks that people back home will go crazy over! Think hippie stuff - chillums, trousers, jewellery, etc. These items will be authentic and dirt cheap. Then, when you are outside that country you can sell the authentic handcrafted Indian peace pipe (that you paid

$.75 cents for in Mumbai) for $15 at festivals or online! It's a great way to make 1,000% or more on your investments.

Busking

Play an instrument? Tap into your inner performer! While not guaranteed, street performing musicians (aka busking) can bring in some good money! Next time you're walking by a street performer, take a look at their tip jar. If the musician chose the right location and is talented enough, there's a pretty good shot they are making some dough! Also, as a musician, you should look into giving lessons while travelling, or playing gigs at bars or hostels. They might give you a free bed or some drinks. Not a bad payoff for a few hours of jammin'!

Travel Nurse

If you are a nurse, or if you are thinking about becoming a nurse, being a travelling nurse is one of the single most amazing careers you can get into. Travelling nurses are usually hired for thirteen to twenty six weeks in whatever location they choose. Housing is usually covered, and due to the high demand and urgency, travelling nurses are paid more than regular nurses. It's one of the best ways to travel and save a stupid amount of money.

Flight Attendant

An oldie but a goodie. Being a flight attendant isn't as glamorous as it once was, but if you are looking to work and travel, this is a fantastic job. Free flights, long stopovers to explore, and the ability to tweak your schedule to have a few weeks off a month - there's a lot to like!

Bollywood extra

A bit more off the cuff, but more than possible! Bollywood is the movie capital of India and puts out *double* the amount of movies Hollywood does per year. A high quantity of movies means a big need for actors, especially foreign actors to fill foreign roles. I've met plenty of people that work and travel while living their acting "dreams" in Bollywood!

New Zealand / Australia work visa

Depending on where you are from, New Zealand and Australia are two of the easiest countries to enter on a work visa. The visa allows you to be employed in most industries, but you'll most likely find work in the food, hospitality, or farming industries. Australia recently reduced their visa fee by $50, and upped the age group from 30 to 35. This is HUGE for anyone who thought they were too old to experience a year of Aussie life, now is your chance.

Farm work in Australia

A backpacker's secret - three months of farm work ("specified work") in Australia gets you a year visa! Sounds great right? It can be but do be careful. While there are many stories of backpackers working on farms that pay them fairly, there are nearly as many that have expressed being exploited and paid unjustly. Not to put you off - the incentive is amazing, just make sure to do your research before you get your farm on!

Sell timeshares

Have you ever been told you are a good salesman? Could you sell shit to a pig? Ice to an Eskimo? A rolling suitcase (come on, they're unbelievably stupid) to me? Selling timeshares (or anything else) is a great way to work and travel.

Overseas companies want to sell tourists on timeshares but have found it more profitable to hire the salesman that can relate to the potential customer. Hence, the timeshare company in Greece wants to hire a Brit to pitch timeshares to Brits visiting Greece on holiday. Got all that? This is certainly not for everyone, but it is a way to travel and make money!

Ski resorts

While I mentioned resorts and seasonal work before, skiing deserves its own holler. Ski resorts are notorious for hiring travellers, often under the table. You won't get paid much and will likely be overworked, but it's a great way to work hard, play hard and make some friends! Plus there will always be skiing perks which are obviously awesome.

Online poker

Thrill seekers, beware! This is not a line of work for everyone. But if you are good at poker and can maintain the discipline required, playing poker can be a great way to work and travel... I rented a flat with a random bunch of backpackers in Medellin and one of the lads there was travelling the world, funding his adventures by playing poker online - he had a system that dictated how much risk he took and how much money he needed to make to maintain his lifestyle.

Join the Peace Corp

A different work and travel experience, the Peace Corp is no joke. It's a two-year commitment, you have very little influence on where you are stationed, and you only get two days off per month. But if you are serious about helping people, this could be the experience of a lifetime. Also, if you are eyeing a particular career, having Peace Corps experience on your resume can be a game changer in certain industries.

Lots of options, right?

The gigs listed above are all viable means of making money. There are a ton of options… This means that you can hone in on your personal skills and find a job that is best suited for you.

Chapter Summary

While money is very important in the travel-game, I want you to know that it's not everything. It is always possible to earn a quick buck, as long as you are willing to hustle and go door to door. Let's review.

- You won't need much money to travel. Yes, you'll need something, but don't think you need to take out a huge loan. Travelling on $10 a day is more than possible.
- Pick a number to save and stick to it! If you don't stick to it you run the risk of putting off your travels. Anything more than $3,000 can last you months, especially if you find some work on the road!

- If you are serious about living a life on the road, sell all the stuff you don't need.
- Sacrificing three boring months at home for nine awesome months of travel is totally worth it.
- Minimizing the crap in your life will help you separate what you need and don't need and better prepare you for the road.
- There are so many jobs to be found while travelling, keep the list as a reminder. A lot of the time, all you have to do to find a job is ask around.

Chapter Five
Broke Backpacker Hacks

We've made it!

This is where everything starts to get juicy. The next few chapters revolve around one thing - the tips, tricks and hacks I learned in my six years of travelling the world broke. In that time, I mastered backpacking on the cheap, which laid the foundation for how to travel the world on $10 a day.

Prepare to learn how to spend practically nothing on accommodation, transport, food and activities all around the world...

Let the magic, begin!

Why Travelling Broke is the Best Adventure

It's hard for me to regret my years travelling the world broke because it was *hands down*, ***without a doubt***, *BAR NONE* - the greatest adventure of my life.

Travelling broke taught me more about travel, more about the world and more about myself than any other experience in the world could have. It will do the same for you.

Travelling without much money both tests and ultimately sharpens your ability to adapt.

While this whole travelling broke thing might sound intense… it's not. It's super fun and usually fairly simple. You'll be shocked just how easy it is to get used to as the rewards make the challenges so worthwhile.

I've spent the majority of my adult life on the road; hitchhiking and camping around the world without any real fixed plans - simply a burning passion to see and experience as much as possible.

Personally, I enjoy the challenge of travelling on a budget, it makes my travels more raw and forces me to interact with people. I've made many lasting friendships through Couchsurfing, I am still in touch with people who I have hitched rides with and I am lucky enough to have friends all over the world.

Would this have been possible if I had been travelling like a flashpacker?

Staying in plush hotels and eating in fancy restaurants aimed at tourists may seem like fun but ultimately you are less likely to really connect with a destination, to get under its skin, to make friends with the people who live there and to actually experience a culture.

Which is what this is all about! Really experiencing a culture. Let's get into it.

Accommodation 101

Sure, you might have a relative living in Lebanon you can crash with, and you'll occasionally be able to crash out on an airport bench but usually the broke backpacker has **four** sleeping options. We'll go from *most* expensive to *least* expensive

AirBnB

You want to talk about a company that revolutionized the way we travel? I have a lot of respect for AirBnB's business model – this is a company that changed everything and quickly became a posterchild for what a 'startup' company can achieve. I like to use AirBnB for a couple of very specific situations.

1. Getting laid
2. Recovering when I'm sick.
3. When you just need to recharge the batteries

Mostly, I recommend AirBnB for two people, when you're looking for some privacy.

Banging in hostels can be tricky and can quickly piss off your dorm amigos. Camping sex can be fun but isn't always comfortable, and whilst I have had a couple of flings with Couchsurfing hosts, you can't exactly have sex in a host's home if the host is not involved!

So AirBnBs are highly recommended for people who want to get naked together. It'll set you back a bit, but not much and certainly not as much as a hotel room.

AirBnB prices are often very reasonable – if you book in advance when you can snap up the best priced rooms.

I'll let you in on a secret though - over the last two years I have racked up over $5000 of AirBnB credit and have stayed in some amazing places without ever having to pay a penny. Sign up to AirBnB today and get $35 free credit using the URL on the last page of the book, you can then invite your buddies and every time anybody joins through your referral link you will earn $35 yourself, this quickly adds up.

Hostels 101

The hostel lifestyle is something that should be experienced by everybody at some point in their travels. Hostels are the epicenter of the independent-travel-universe. You won't always need to stay in hostels (couchsurfing and camping are two cheaper means of accommodation), but staying in hostels can give you a great opportunity to make friends and team up with other independent travellers.

Aside from the social perks, the second biggest draw to staying in hostels is the cost. Whilst hostels can be expensive (cough; Western Europe), the cost of dorm beds in some parts of the world are shockingly cheap and hostels are always cheaper than hotels.

Hostels are cheap

You can find hostels for less than $7 USD a night in Eastern Europe, $6 USD in India, and $3 a night in Cambodia.

Now you might be thinking, "Wait, $7 a night for a hostel, that's 70% of my daily budget Will!"

Yes, for the broke traveler, a mere $7 hostel bed can run you back, which is why to make the $10 a day goal work, you'll have to either avoid hostels by camping and Couchsurfing, see if you can score a free bed in exchange for 'help' or only stay in hostels when you can find a real steal of a price.

Working in hostels

Helping out in hostels is a great way to stretch your bucks as you normally get a free bed and sometimes free food and booze. Most long-term travellers have picked up work in hostels at one point or another and honestly, hostel work can be a lot of fun, especially if you get to be the cool gunslinger, or gunslinger-ess, serving drinks behind the bar.

Hostels hire backpackers to do some of the cleaning, mind reception and run the bar.

Sometimes, if you stay in an area for a long time, you might be asked to run activities organised through the hostel - like walking tours or, more likely, pub crawls - this can be a good way to boost your income as you normally get to keep tips at the end.

Working in hostels is normally very casual, when you find work at a hostel you are not technically 'employed' by the hostel… it's more like coming to 'an agreement' with the hostel. You help them out (minding the bar), they help you out (free bed and breakfast!). It's a win win.

Working in hostels is a lot less like work and a lot more like hanging out and bullshitting with other travellers. If you're working on the bar you serve a couple beers, chat up the other travellers (backpacker grapevine), and maybe have a drink or two yourself.

Hostel life is what you make of it. If you want to meet a lot of people, go out on pub crawls and find some bartending work - hostels are for you!

My one issue with hostels is that travellers who stay exclusively in hostels can get a bit sucked into the party scene and end up seeing very little of the area because they are constantly raving at their hostel.

The good thing about hostels is that there are many, many options out there and whilst party hostels are fairly common you can also find quieter options with chilled gardens or common areas.

Camping 101

A fantastic alternative to sleeping in a hostel is camping out in the great outdoors... Camping gives you time to properly soak in your environment and the opportunity to see some truly stunning night skies.

Not to mention, it is almost always free to camp. While you can choose to pay to camp at a campsite... you never need to. Just walk into the woods, find a patch of flat land and you've found home sweet home!

I've saved thousands of dollars by camping while travelling the world. Having a tent enables you to spend nothing on lodging, inching you closer and closer to the magical $10-a-day number. Best of all, having a tent means you have a lot more options when on the road – you don't need to worry so much about finding a place to sleep because, heck, you have a home in your pack.

You should especially consider camping if travelling to developed countries – without a tent, travelling on a budget through Western Europe or North America becomes truly difficult.

Camping is usually an amazing experience, but it is not without its setbacks.

The biggest disadvantage is the initial cost. Camping gear comes in all prices, but in my experience a tent and sleeping bag are the last things you want to skimp on. Bad camping gear is almost worse than no camping gear.

Poor quality camping gear will eventually result in some truly terrible sleep – whether it's being too cold, too hot, soaked to the skin or eaten alive by bugs. If you buy a cheap ass tent, it will eventually break.

The second obvious disadvantage is that camping gear is bulky and heavy.

Sometimes, it's real heavy. Lightweight camping gear is a smart option, but will double the cost of your initial investment.

Whilst we are budget travellers and pride ourselves in cutting costs, skimping on a tent is just a bad idea.

Tents aren't super expensive. A proper tent will cost you less than $200 USD and should last a lifetime.

You can normally pick up a solid tent for around the $150 mark, maybe a little less. For this kind of price, you should be able to pick up a high quality tent – not the kind of thing you could survive in on Everest, but the kind of thing which will serve the average nomad very well indeed. In my opinion, that's $150 well spent.

For more info on tents, check out thebrokebackpacker. com/best-backpacking-tent/ where I break down all the options.

If you are travelling through Central America and the average hostel is $8 a night, that means that after a mere nineteen nights, your tent will have paid for itself.

So think about how much money you'll save over years, or a lifetime of travel!

Spend $150 on the tent, and then get a decent roll mat for $10. The roll mat will provide some comfort and help keep you warm as it'll insulate you from the ground. If you have a tent and roll mat, you can often survive without a sleeping bag, depending on the climate. I emphasize sometimes. You can usually pick up a sleeping bag fairly cheap and if you have a good quality tent and a rollmat to separate you from the cold ground, it's OK to scrimp on this.

Pros of camping

- Save a ton of money
- One of a kind experience in the wild
- Closer to nature and away from the noise
- Amazing alone time
- Quite romantic if you're not alone

Cons of camping

- High initial cost
- Some potential maintenance costs
- So. Damn. Heavy.

Camping tips

The main thing with camping is to ensure that you pick a flat spot that isn't near a river. Flash-floods catch people out every year and trust me, there is nothing worse than waking up in the middle of the night to find your tent is suddenly in the middle of a river and all your gear is ruined.

Ideally, you want to choose a spot sheltered from the wind as well and it makes sense to find something a little secluded as often you will be camping in a spot where you technically shouldn't be - the chances of getting discovered are extremely low, just don't be ultra-visible.

Always carry a headtorch when you go camping, it'll be worth its weight in gold!

The money you can save and the experiences camping out in the wild are without rival. But you need to understand that it isn't something you half ass.

So give it a go, but do it right. Get a bit of experience at home. Borrow a tent from a friend or family member, go to the woods and familiarize yourself with how to put it up and take it down. The worst way to learn how to camp for the first time is on the road in some dark forest… Know how to set up your tent *before* you actually *need* to set it up.

So heed my advice, if you are the outdoorsy type and the camping lifestyle suits you, buck up and spend the money. The investment will be well worth it.

Couchsurfing 101

Couchsurfing. Otherwise known as my secret sauce. Other-otherwise known as how I've saved tens of thousands of dollars on accommodation while travelling the world.

Whilst Couchsurfing is a great backpacker secret, it's not much of a secret. There are 14 million people actively registered on the website, and the community is growing every day.

Couchsurfing is most popular in developed countries. The below numbers were found and verified through multiple sources.

1. U.S.A. - 900,000 users
2. Germany - 400,000 users
3. France - 350,000 users
4. England - 200,000 users
5. Canada - 160,000 users
6. Spain - 130,000 users
7. Italy - 130,000 users
8. Brazil - 110,000 users
9. Australia - 110,000 users
10. China - 95,000 users

That's a lot of couches!

But here's the cool bit - while the expensive countries have the most registered users, *Couchsurfing is now active in nearly every country in the world!* While it's a bit more popular in Western nations, there are Couchsurfing opportunities everywhere. I've surfed well over a hundred times and hosted about thirty Couchsurfers in various digs around the world...

Couchsurfing safety

The history of Couchsurfing is actually pretty interesting. What started as a grassroots movement in 1999 has now become a for-profit corporation that is aiming for an IPO in the next few years.

Over this time, the site has gone from a casual "hey you can sleep on my couch!" to a stricter system that boasts accountability.

All surfers and hosts are greatly encouraged to spend $20 a year to use CS but, when signing up, it's possible to skip this (keep an eye out in the bottom left on one of the signup pages, there's a way round it...).

In general Couchsurfing is very safe. There have been a small number (five in my research) of horror stories with Couchsurfing over the past 17 years. While the crimes were terrible, because of Couchsurfing profile process and accountability - the criminals have all been caught and sentenced to prison.

Ok. Whoa. This is getting dark.

Let's take it back a step.

So while there have been a handful of bad things that have happened in Couchsurfing, we are talking 5ish events in 17 years spread out over millions of millions of millions of hosts and surfers.

In other words, the chances of something bad happening to you when Couchsurfing is the same chances of getting mauled by a gorilla at the zoo (RIP Harambe). Couchsurfing is possibly the safest way to get free accommodation when backpacking on a budget.

Couchsurfing as a safety net

When I travelled to Venezuela, everybody warned me I was a fool; to travel in Venezuela was to risk robbery and murder, kidnap and bribery.

I took to South America anyway, figuring I would get some more up to date info on the ground; surely I would meet a backpacker who had been, or a Venezuelan, who could tell me more about what it was actually like within the country. I never met another backpacker outside of Venezuela who had been to Venezuela; the general consensus was that it was just too dangerous.

Slowly but surely I bumped into a few Venezuelans, their reactions were less than encouraging.

"Are you crazy man!? My country is dangerous even for us, and you can't speak Spanish!"

"Don't do it, you will get killed for sure"

"I left my country because it is too dangerous, you would be stupid to go to Venezuela"

Little did all these naysayers know that I had a secret weapon. I had a tried and tested way of getting around dangerous countries safely…

Couchsurfing.

Couchsurfing attracts a certain kind of person; the kind of

person who is proud of their country and wants to welcome visitors properly. The kind of person who wants to ensure you have the best possible time whilst adventuring, the kind of person who will go out of their way to make sure you are safe.

The feedback from Venezuelan immigrants had freaked me out a little bit. Maybe, just maybe, Venezuela was going to be different – perhaps even Couchsurfing could not keep me safe in 'lawless' Venezuela?

I took to the internet and scrolled throw a half dozen profiles before I found somebody who lived near the Colombian border and looked like fun.

Esthela was studying at university and had hosted another backpacker before me, a German chap, one of Venezuela's few visitors. As soon as I had reached out to her she had ecstatically responded that she would love to host me and began telling me tales of her previous adventures with her German friend.

I spoke to Esthela about all that I had heard of Venezuela, my concerns about visiting and she responded kindly that "Yes, Venezuela is more dangerous than other South American countries but it is not as bad as people say. If you come, I can help you with advice to keep you safe".

It was all I needed to hear; sure, I reckoned backpacking in Venezuela was going to be a challenge, perhaps one of the most 'dangerous' countries I was ever to visit, but I knew that it would be worth the risk – for I would have all of Venezuela's steaming jungles, towering peaks and abundant wildlife to myself – all I had to do was get there.

Venezuela was and is a country in turmoil. Corruption is rampant, inflation is spiraling out of control and there are more kidnappings than in any other country. Luckily, I had Esthela to show me the ropes.

She eased me into Venezuelan life by explaining that, in general, it's not a great idea to go out exploring when it's dark. I took this on board and over the next few days began to plan my Venezuelan adventure… It would not be easy, I would have to navigate long journeys, pesky language barriers and steaming jungle.

Esthela offered to put me in touch with friends she had along the way who could look after me and, after a few days, I said a grateful thank you to her family and continued on my journey.

Venezuela was a total blast; I conquered the highest table top mountain in the world, Mt Roraima, partied in the student capital of Merida with it's 8 cent beers and beautiful women and explored the vast wetland plains by horseback and 4×4. I was one of very few backpackers in the area and, as a result, I had all of these amazing experiences purely to myself.

This is what couchsurfing does. It puts you in contact with locals who know the area, want you to enjoy it, and will tell you exactly how to do it safely. This is why I highly recommend using Couchsurfing for "dodgier" parts of the world. It can actually keep you safer!

Squatting 101

The cheapest option. No signup. No doing dishes as a nice gesture. No tent investment. Squatting is when you enter and sleep in an abandoned building. There are a lot of squatting communities, especially throughout Europe, with the most famous being Free Town Christiania in Denmark.

I have squatted a few times, usually in very dilapidated, very obviously uninhabited, buildings I've stumbled across whilst looking for a place to camp.

Squatting is illegal and I don't advise making it a regular part of your travels however there are many great permanent squats set up around Europe, usually with communities of artists and musicians and hippies living inside, so these can be well worth visiting as you pass through.

Often, if you are polite and on a similar wavelength, you will be invited to stay a night or two!

Accommodation Summary

While other lodging options exist (hotels, etc) you're going to want to steer clear of them. By using a healthy mix of Couchsurfing, camping, hostels, and the occasional steamy night at an AirBnB, you'll save tens of thousands of dollars and have a far better experience.

Give each option a shot! While I love camping, it's nice to get my social on and drop in a hostel every now and then, or say screw it and squat somewhere. It's all a part of the experience baby!

Transport 101

So you know how to find places to sleep, but now how the hell are you supposed to get around?

Broke backpackers usually have two options - local transportation and hitchhiking.

Local Transport 101

While local transit might run up quite a bill in large

Western cities (London, New York, etc) you will be shocked how cheap local transport is in developing countries. I'm talking bus rides and train rides that will get you exactly where you need to be and will cost mere pennies.

Using local transit is crucial to saving money while travelling, and is yet another fantastic way to experience your travels like a local.

When I first went to India, I travelled exclusively by local buses and local trains; riding in the cheapest carriages with 300 Indians packed to bursting. I rarely saw other foreigners in these carriages and on my later visits to India I started to ride on the AC coaches as they were significantly more comfortable and not much more expensive.

India's extremely cheap public transport allowed me to travel tens of thousands of kilometers for just a few dollars. I once endured a thirty three hour train journey, travelling from Rajahstan to Goa via some middle of nowhere town.

I had a nine hour wait (but I met up with a Couchsurfer for breakfast so it was all good). It was a truly crazy journey, and I went a bit stir-crazy sharing a bunk meant for one person with four Indians but heck, it got me from one end of the country to the other and it cost less than ten bucks!

Obviously this is an extreme example and there are often multiple different levels of local transport available; you don't always have to take the cheapest one - simply by travelling on local transport rather than booking your train or bus ticket through an agency promising a 'tourist grade vehicle' will help you save money.

Always catch the night bus / train

Another travel-veteran trick - the night bus/train!

Some bus excursions are terrible - I've done this one route in Pakistan four times now. A horrific, ass-bruising, 17 hour winding bus journey. This particular bus route has ten army checkpoints meaning it's impossible to get any sleep. The army is always so shocked to see a foreigner that they usually insist on sharing a cup of chai.

This particular journey is not for the faint-hearted, but some overnight bus excursions are very pleasant indeed with many countries now offering comfortable coaches with decent seats or even sleeping bunks - if you want to save a bit more money while travelling, this is a great way to double dip.

Let's say you're travelling from Port Elizabeth, South Africa to Cape town. You could catch the nine hour bus at 11am bus OR take the nine our bus at 11pm bus.

If you're smart, you'll take the night bus. Then your bus morphs into a budget travel friendly combo of transport and bed. Get on the bus late, bundle up, pop in some headphones, and sleep soundly.

Then, you get to wake up in your new destination, you saved money on your ticket (night fares are cheaper) and you saved money on accommodation that night!

Hitchhiking 101

The first time I stood on the side of the road I was scared. My anxiety was through the god-damn roof.

I was a relatively shy kid and the idea of throwing my backpack into some unknown person's car and then asking them for something for free, a lift, made me feel uncomfortable.

Still, I was far more scared of remaining in England, of getting a job I hated to pay off a mortgage for a house I didn't want (or have).

So I packed a bag, stood by the side of the road... and I stuck out my thumb.

My first ever lift was an older Polish lady who drove me nearly fifty miles out of her way to drop me near the coast where I caught a ride on a boat headed to France. Sensing, perhaps, that I was a little uneasy, she talked non-stop, chatting about how she used to hitchhike a lot as a girl in Poland but had not seen anybody trying to hitchhike before in England.

She asked me where I was going and I remember answering *'further than France'* but thinking *'I have no idea'*.

Hitchhiking is a fantastic experience and one of the oldest methods of Backpacker travel out there. There is something intoxicating about rocking up to a lay-by, sticking out your thumb and seeing where the road takes you.

My first hitchhiking journeys in Europe are still some of my fondest travel memories... I didn't take a phone, just half a dozen books to read, and I camped most nights. It was simple. I enjoyed the daily routine of waking up, cooking some beans on my stove and making my way to the road to try and catch another ride going further East.

Fast forward nine years and I've hitched on four continents, racked up tens of thousands of miles and caught hundreds of rides.

Hitchhiking has been a highlight of my travels and I've had some incredible experiences that have only been possible because I was hitchhiking. I hitched from England to Africa, from France to Romania, from Albania to Azerbaijan; multi-month hitchhiking expeditions that forced me to step out of my comfort zone, to meet amazing people and to get to grips with the local culture.

I met my future wife in Iran and we fell in love whilst hitchhiking across the country together, crossing into Pakistan and then India – all through the power of the thumb.

Hitchhiking is, simply, one of the best ways to get around the globe and to actually connect with amazing people whilst travelling. Some of the most interesting, unbelievable, shocking and inspiring conversations I've had have been with random folks who have picked me up from the side of the street.

Hitchhiking has been around for decades and was first made popular in the times of the hippies. As a kid, I read *On The Road* by Jack Kerouac (a hero of mine) and was inspired to try living the hitchhiker-bum life myself. Hitchhiking is perfect for broke backpackers as it's a free way to get from A to B...

So, how exactly do you hitch a ride? Are there any good hitchhiking websites you can check out? Is hitchhiking legal? Read on amigo to find out everything you need to know about hitchhiking...

Top Tips for Happy Hitching

Be flexible, be happy: hitchhiking is a great way to save money but you have to realise that hitchhiking often makes it impossible to plan when and where you will turn up. You need to be flexible, enjoy the ride and accept that sometimes you will have to wait a while to get picked up. If you look approachable and happy you are far more likely to get a ride, make sure you are not wearing sunglasses or a cap covering your face, eye contact is key!

Take lots of pens: I am a fan of big, simple signs (usually with just one word such as 'South' or a road code like M6) when hitchhiking and although you can often find cardboard or other junk to use as a sign, you need to have a pen handy.

Take the right equipment: If you are hitchhiking any real distance you must be prepared to spend the night under the stars. Sometimes drivers will offer you a place to stay in their house but you cannot rely on this, take a tent and make sure you have lots of warm gear as well as a good map.

Hitching and camping are two peas in a pod. If you're doing one, you almost certainly need to be doing the other. Camping gives you access to a lot more peace of mind when hitching a ride. Which situation would you rather be in?

1. Trying to hitch a ride to the next town, knowing that if it gets dark before you get a lift you will have to walk until you reach some sign of civilisation.

Or

2. Trying to hitch a ride to the next town, knowing that if it gets dark before you get a lift you'll simply pitch your tent for the night and settle on down.

Number two sounds significantly better. Having a tent is essential if hitching, it gives you so much more flexibility and when travelling, flexibility is everything. The more flexible you can be, the less stressed you will get.

Use your imagination: You can hitch literally anywhere in the world, obviously some areas are more dangerous than others but it can be done. There are no limits to the amount of awesome adventures you could have hitchhiking.

Pick your hitching spot carefully: I tend to go for a lay-by on a long straight road or a service station. If you are not getting picked up do not be afraid to walk down the road a bit and find somewhere better to hitch from. Basically you need to find a spot where drivers are naturally forced to slow down.

Be polite and friendly: Once your driver has pulled over, run up to them – do not make them wait. Thank them for stopping and find out if they are going in the right direction, even if they aren't make sure to say thanks properly before they leave.

Once in the car shake their hand and tell them your name as well as asking theirs. A lot of the time drivers pick up hitchers because they are bored and want a distraction, they will probably expect you to make small talk with them.

Do not do anything in the car, e.g. eating, smoking, rolling down the windows, without first asking the driver's' permission. Try to negotiate where you will be dropped off before you arrive, you do not want to end up in a dodgy area or the middle of a big town when you could have found yourself on a nice straight road instead.

Utilise online resources: My favourite hitchhiking resource is Hitchwiki as it has a fantastic database of quality hitching spots for all over the world. It really is a fantastic website and I highly recommend using it to help plan your route or to get advice if you are stuck somewhere. Another great place to get decent info is the hitchhiking forum on Couchsurfing.

Stay safe: *If someone gives you a bad vibe do not get in the car with them.*

*At the risk of annoying feminists everywhere I am going to voice my opinion that **women should avoid hitchhiking alone.***

A boy and girl combo will get the most lifts. If you need to find a hitchhiking buddy this is relatively easy thanks to Hitchhiker Facebook Groups.

Is hitchhiking legal?

Hitchhiking is legal in most countries, including the USA, but you can get in trouble if you try hitching from somewhere stupid – like a motorway. In general, avoid trying to flag down cars that are travelling super fast and instead find a gas station or layby where cars can easily stop to pick you up.

Is hitchhiking fun?

Hell yes, it's simply the best way to get around if you are broke and is possible pretty much everywhere.

Transport summary

You'll probably have to catch a flight or two, and an expensive train ride here and there can be nice, but if you want to travel on a budget - you gotta hitch and ride like a local.

Doing so will keep your transit cost to mere pennies, and will enable you to have a much more authentic and local experience with far superior stories to tell to mates down the line.

Food 101

Personally I find the challenge of eating cheap while travelling pretty fun. While not always a guarantee, the cuisines that are the cheapest are the most delicious. And the expensive, watered down, bland crap catered to tourists is usually just that… crap.

The more you travel the better you get at finding good cheap food, but let me fill you in on a couple of tips.

1. Follow the locals

This is far and away the most important bit of information I can give you. If you spot a hole in the wall restaurant or food stand packed with locals - you need to eat there.

Ladies and gentlemen, this is for one reason. Locals from developing nations don't mess around when it comes to their food. They eat cheap. They eat quick. But most importantly, they eat good.

Most cultures in developing nations have proud origins in their food. Think Thai, Moroccan, Turkish, Peruvian, Mexican, Vietnamese, Indian, Persian. These are some of the most renowned cuisines on the planet, and when you are in these countries, if you follow the locals you will rejoice in a wonderland of affordable delicious flavors.

The counter to this point is if you are following the locals, avoid the tourists.

Tourist restaurants are the freaking worst. They cater to bland Western palates and charge exorbitant amounts of money for this "food". You can get some twice as delicious for half the price if you look just a little longer.

2. Eat street food

Again, if you're a bit nervous about food, then make sure it's a busy stall (but I do emphasize, this is only meant to keep your fears at bay). Why would locals willingly eat at a venue that gets people sick? The answer is, they wouldn't. Also, they're probably eating there because it's delicious **and** cheap.

3. Work Exchanges

Work exchanges will come up continuously in this guide because... they rock. You can exchange work for food just about anywhere, and with programs like WWOOF, HelpX or hostel work, you can put a serious dent in the cost of feeding yourself.

Another backpacker trick is to ask restaurants if they need help. It's a different type of work exchange, often done in the spur of the moment. If you notice the restaurant is extremely busy, see if they need a hand. If they say yes, you can score a free meal.

Side note - this works pretty well in Europe, but wherever you try, make sure it's local restaurant. You'll have more luck at a ma and pop type pub than a McDonald's. Smell what I'm cooking?

I want to make a point here - please do not underestimate how important it is to eat cheap.

I'm not suggesting eating unhealthy, in fact as you'll see in the next chapter, eating healthy is the next cheapest thing you can do. But you need to ensure you are looking for low cost options.

Reason being, we might be able to get away with no booze. Or we can hitchhike and Couchsurf everywhere and never pay for accommodation.

But no matter what, you're going to have to eat 2-3 square meals a day, every day for the rest of your life.

If you average $5 a meal and eat 20 meals a week, that's $100 a week on food. That's $5,200 a year you are spending on food while travelling.

What if you could cut that down to $3 a meal? $3,120 a year. Shedding the extra two bucks a meal saves you over $2,000 a year.

Don't starve yourself, don't eat rubbish, don't have personal hunger strikes to protest against high restaurant prices. Just make efforts to find cheaper alternatives. If you pay attention, you'll notice you'll develop some spidey sixth sense where you'll be able to pick good cheap restaurants with your eyes closed.

Making the conscious effort will really pay off in the long run.

But arguably the best food-tip I can give you is to….

Cook Your Own Food!

No matter where in the world you are, as long as you have access to a kitchen, you will always be able to lower food costs by hitting up a market and cooking your own food.

A huge draw to hostels, hostels, AirBnB and Couchsurfing is having access to a kitchen.

But just because you're cooking your own food in a kitchen doesn't automatically mean you are saving money. Eat cheap and eat smart. **Remember, food is fuel**.

To me, cooking for yourself isn't *just* a good idea, it's **imperative**. While cheap local food can be delicious, in some parts of the world it isn't always the healthiest option.

Our bodies need fruits and veggies. It is a biological fact. Fruits and veggies = vitamins and minerals. It's science.

And some local cuisines don't really serve much on the side of veggies. Some countries in Asia are veggie friendly (India, Thailand) but others seem to have an exclusive love for meat and carbs.

Or maybe you had Burger King for breakfast *and* lunch, so maybe it's time to try something new for dinner.

Bring on the cooking. Go to the local mart. Buy some produce. Unleash your inner Anthony Bourdain. You'll feel amazing.

You can cook at your hostel or couchsurfing host's

kitchen. Or if you are camping, you will hopefully have a stove with you.

Veggies are usually cheap. It doesn't matter where in the world you go, you can buy peppers, broccoli, onions, garlic, white mushrooms, cabbage and carrots for next to nothing.

$10 A DAY

Eating Guide

FOOD IS FUEL

While eating delicious is a priority, remember that you need to fuel your body with nutrients to effectively travel the world

EAT LOCAL

Follow the locals - look for high volume restaurants. They will likely be cheap and delicious

FIND STREET FOOD

Cheap as f**k - street food is a staple for budget travel

COOK YOURSELF

Utilizing a kitchen (hostel, couchsurfing, AirBnb) or cooking while camping are must do's. Produce is cheap and lasts for a few meals

SNACK SMART

Don't munch on crisps. Nuts, fruits, dried fruits and cheese are high in nutrition, last a while, and are fairly affordable

www.TheBrokeBackpacker.com

Trail mix is a backpacker's best friend. It will last forever, and is full of nutrients… probably. In places like Iran and Pakistan it's dirt cheap to make your own trail mix.

Pasta and veggies are ridiculously easy to make and always tasty. Cold pasta salad can last days.

Instant noodles are always cheap, but try and spruce it up with an egg (protein) and some kale (nutrients).

I always travel with a pocket-rocket, a small camping stove that lets me cook basic food and boil water for tea or coffee in the mornings. This is one of the most valuable things in my pack and I truly enjoy the flexibility it offers me.

Say No to Sickness

The food aspect of travel can really intimidate people, but the good news is it doesn't need to. Your body is surprisingly tough and if you do get sick, you *will* bounce back.

Don't get me wrong, on my travels I've battled food poisoning, unending traveller's diarrhea and mystery meat but most of the time, I'm fine. I like food but for me it's fuel, it's necessary to keep me going and if it doesn't taste great? I don't really care… I'm backpacking the world baby!

When in doubt; 'boil it, peel it, cook it, or forget it' - a good mantra to live by if you want to avoid getting sick.

Dumpster Diving

Dumpster diving is the act of taking advantage of the wastefulness of developed nations, by going through dumpsters and finding things that should not have been tossed.

Hear me out, if you've never heard of it, it's probably not

as gross as you're envisioning.

People dumpster dive for many things (and some have found loot worth thousands of dollars) but often travellers will check out the dumpsters behind supermarkets for food that has been thrown out because it is past it's sell by date... pretty often, this food is still good to eat.

What dumpster diving doesn't mean - Diving from a high board into a pile of trash.

What dumpster diving does mean - finding a corporate restaurant in the USA or Australia that is tossing out perfectly good food that you just collect around back.

Dumpster diving works best when you're staying somewhere a while as you can find regular opportunities and maybe even make friends with somebody who throws all this stuff away and get them to leave it out for you.

Food Summary

Eat well, eat cheap, and eat healthy. The whole point of eating is to nourish our bodies, but don't feel the need to sacrifice quality because of it. There's a healthy medium you can hit!

Eat street food, cook like a boss and always keep a bag of trail mix around – it's damn delicious.

Haggling 101

The last of the Broke Backpacker hacks, but arguably the most important.

When you hit the road for the first time, learning how to

haggle is pretty damn important...

In some countries, haggling isn't really a part of the culture but when backpacking in places like India, if you don't learn how to haggle you will often find yourself paying ten times more than you should.

So, if you're keen to learn how to travel cheap around the world, learning how to haggle is a pretty massive part of it and will help you stretch your funds as far as possible. In most countries (especially Asia and South America) there is a 'local rate' and a 'foreigner rate'. These rates are very ingrained in local culture and to them it's OK to try and rip off foreigners.

Most decent human beings will instantly drop the price once they realise that you know they are asking for too much, but some bastards will always continue trying to rip you off - usually in places like India or Morocco.

Haggling becomes increasingly important when you are trying to buy something like a souvenir, a tour or a room for the night and simply don't know how much you should pay, in general I like to pay about 30% of the starting price assuming that I'm in a country where I know I am being quoted higher pricing on account of being perceived as a 'rich foreigner'.

Top Tips for Masterful Haggling

Local cash: Make sure you have the right money before you start negotiating. Locals will never give you a good exchange rate as this is a simple way for them to make more money out of you. It is usually worth having local money and some USD/Euros as well, occasionally you can get a better rate for dollars than for local currency. Make sure you have a good understanding of what the local currency is worth.

Research: If you know what you want to buy then it makes sense to ask around and see what other travellers have paid for similar items. Make sure to ask for stall recommendations and about other travellers' own haggling experiences in the area. Know what you want to pay and then aim for ten to twenty percent less for that when haggling. Always start below your preferred final price when haggling.

Language: Do not get angry but do stay assertive, avoid the use of "umm". Even when you think someone is taking the piss with prices it usually is not a good idea to get angry. Learning a few phrases and some numbers in the local language can be extremely helpful and will help you get a better deal especially if you can say things like "This is too expensive". Rather than saying things like "Is X amount ok?" instead use phrases such as "OK I'll give you X amount as that seems fair to me".

Stay Calm: Do not get too excited, act nonchalant and be honest; do you really need a massive, camel leather, lamp? OK, so you don't need one but you do want one providing the price is right. The best way to get a good price is to pretend you don't really want the lamp, indifference can work wonders. Try walking away after entering negotiations; the price will magically plummet.

Take your time: Often I will haggle for the same product with two or three vendors, I will see what the absolute lowest price I can get is from all three and then go for the cheapest one and try to knock another 10% off. When you enter a store or a market make sure to have a look around. Usually there are lots of identical products on sale with the most expensive being at the stalls with the best location, go deeper into the market for fewer customers and better deals. Make sure to inspect your chosen product carefully, if you find flaws and point them out this can usually lower the price.

Do NOT ask for the price straight away: Pretend you are browsing and do not ask for the price, after a while the vendor will say something like "Very good price my friend" , you can then ask how much it is without seeming particularly interested.

Body language: One of my favourite techniques is to nod and stick out my hand for a deal ending handshake when I suggest my final price in order to get the vendor to agree with me, beware however the vendor will often try this same technique on you as well!

Bulk purchases: If you intend on buying several of the same thing haggle one down as low as possible first and then try and get a further discount for buying multiple items.

Keep your money hidden: Showing off a wallet stuffed full of cash is never a good idea, I tend to have a pocket of smaller bills easily accessible for small purchases. If you need to get out more money from your wallet turn your back to the vendor and if possible face a wall, this will not be considered rude.

You should not get the 'local price': Ultimately even broke backpackers tend to have a little bit more money than most of the locals in third world countries, I don't have a problem with driving a really hard bargain in a proper shop or from a tour company but if you are buying something small from somebody operating over a stall or out of a small shop then do not try to screw them out of every cent of profit. It seems fair to pay the local price plus ten to fifteen percent however it is definitely not fair to pay some of the ridiculous prices that vendors will often ask in places like India.

Haggling is Important

But it will certainly vary based where in the world you are. If you are somewhere where haggling is acceptable, get some practice in! The ancient art of haggling takes time, practice and patience... Happy haggling amigos!

Booking online or offline?

Sometimes there are things we can't haggle. So the best thing to do is to arrive in a new destination with a hostel already booked. The best way is a healthy combination of the two.

I tend to book offline most of the time as this is when you can haggle however it's worth pointing out that for some places, like Myanmar or Goa, you NEED to book online if you hope to get affordable accommodation.

I always try to sort my first two nights in a new location in advance – sometimes I book a hostel online, other times I make sure I have a Couchsurfing host lined up. After a couple of days, I'm all good and I feel happy winging it.

Other Random Tips

1. Drinking is, for better or worse, a big part of backpacker culture in Asia, so be sure to keep costs down and fit in a 7/11 road-beer where possible!

2. If you want weed, ask bartenders or hostel staff, they will usually tell you if it's possible or too dodgy to pick up in this area.

3. If you are going to buy drugs or get involved in any

dodgy activity, take a buddy. Drug deals can go shady, so the best course of action is to go with back up. I am not recommending you get stuck into this side of things whilst backpacking but, well, you might so if you're going to do it, play it smart.

4. Wear your wallet in your front pocket. It's uncomfortable, but back-pocket wallets are a pickpocket's wet dream. Too easy.

5. Have a stash of emergency cash hidden away - I always have a couple of hundred bucks very well hidden in a specially designed security belt – nope, not a money belt, this is way more subtle than that. Check out the blog to see what I'm talking about.

Chapter Summary

- Travelling broke is the greatest adventure possible, and there are so many ways to make it work on the road.
- For accommodation, you're going to want to tap into camping, couchsurfing and hostels. These are the cheapest options. Feel free to take an occasional AirBnB pass for those special nights
- Hostel life is fun and social. You can meet lots of people, go on organised pub crawls and have a merry time. Sometimes the lack of privacy and surplus of people can be overwhelming, but for the price, hostels are usually on point.
- Camping is free, wild and awesome – just be sure to properly invest in your gear.
- I highly recommend trying out Couchsurfing. It's free

and provides a unique experience and look into your new area. Be courteous to your host - offer to do the dishes or bring a small gift – postcards and fridge magnets go down well. It's a small gesture but it goes a long way.

- Squat if you have to, it's an option.
- Transport is done best when it's cheap or free. I recommend sticking to local transportation (buses and trains when they are affordable) and hitchhiking the rest of the way.
- Hitchhiking is very safe and probably my highest travelling recommendation in general - everybody should try it once. It's extremely liberating to stand on the side of the road with your thumb out like a wanderer of old and hitching offers new experiences and meetings you never would have normally had.
- Eating cheap is easy, but be mindful to eat healthy. This is done best by utilizing a kitchen often and picking up cheap local produce from the market. It'll keep you fit and cost you pennies.
- Carry a pocket-rocket so you can cook your own food.

Chapter Six
Travel Gear

A lot of people really like to nerd out on travel gear. Personally, I believe it's way too easy to end up carrying too much stuff and I prefer to travel light… However, there are definitely some travel essentials which every backpacker should have.

Travel Light as a Feather

Sometimes when on the road, you will see people travelling with so much gear that you wonder how they have retained their sanity. I'm not talking a bit of gear, I'm talking a lot of gear…

Three backpacks, the first HUGE one hugging their back like a large chimpanzee, a second middle sized one straddling their front, and a third bag being dragged around like a baby seal.

And while I really try not to, I usually end up chuckling a bit to myself.

I'm not an asshole, most of the time. It's not the pain they are in that amuses me (but you better believe it's physically straining and exhausting to carry that much stuff around). It's just that I know they could have made do with a third of what they brought.

Usually, after a few days of lugging that much stuff up and down the street, they know it too.

But by this point – they are committed to carrying around enough clothes to dress a small marching band.

We talked about minimalism earlier. Go Japanese again and travel light! It's one of the best pieces of advice I can give you.

How to Travel Light

Funnily, most people think they *want* to travel light. They like the idea in theory. They think to themselves, "I'm only going to bring what I need!"

And then the time comes to pack. And suddenly the idea of leaving this and that behind seems impossible… The gear pile gets bigger and the bag gets heavier. It may seem OK at the time but just you wait till you're out on the road – you will regret packing so much shit.

"But if I bring this drone with me I can get the sickest travel footage ever!"

Touche. You may be right. But does it really matter how sick the travel footage is if two weeks later your Mary Popkins sized suitcase (more on suitcases in a moment) drives you to the point of madness.

You don't need a DSLR, video camera, GoPro, drone and a point and shoot.

You don't need 16 shirts, three pairs of jeans, and four pairs of shoes to make sure you have colour coordinated outfits.

Unless you're getting well and truly off the beaten track,

you won't be needing a mosquito net, trekking boots or a sleeping bag. Pack light, it's the smart move.

TRAVEL LIGHT

Why minimalism is the right choice for backpacking

HEAT

Carrying a big backpack can get pretty damn hot. You'll quickly become annoyed as the sweat accumulates...

LESS BULLSHIT

Lugging backpacks around on buses, airplanes, stairs, hostels, walking is a pain in the ass - Plus you stick out like a sore thumb, try to avoid this.

SAFETY

While theft isn't likely, the more stuff you have, the more of a target you are. Keeping bags light keeps attention off you

EXTRA SPACE

You are going to pick up stuff while on the road. Books from other travelers, necessities for certain excursions and of course a gift for mum!

CHEAPER

Airplanes are starting to charge for carry ons, etc. Instead of needing to buy another second bag, you can just keep filling your current one!

www.TheBrokeBackpacker.com

129

Backpack vs. Suitcase

While I try to be as open minded as possible, I'll never understand why anyone would go backpacking with a suitcase.

There's a reason everyone refers to travelling the world on a budget as "backpacking" and not "suitcasing".

For the love of Buddha - do not take a suitcase, and do not EVER take one of those ridiculous rolling ones. If you do insist on taking a rolling one, please take it somewhere with a ton of cobblestone streets (Prague is nice) and then send me a video of yourself going up a hill… it'll make my day.

There's a time and a place for everything. If you're on a long business trip, going in and out of cabs, checking into snazzy hotels, loaded with bell boys that will take your stuff for you - sure. Get a rolling suitcase. Knock yourself out.

But you're here to travel light, and see the world on a budget.

You want to go backpacking.

Buy a backpack.

What You Need to Spend Money on

We're travelling cheap, but we're not travelling thick. Take the time to do some proper research into the gear you need, to try on a pack or two and then seriously consider investing properly into your gear.

Finding the Right Backpack

Your backpack is going to be your best friend. It's going to be your husband / wife. It's going to be your lover. It's going to be your everything.

So, while I'm an advocate of backpacking on the cheap... there are things that you need to splash some cash on and your backpack is one of them.

If you don't invest in your gear, you will constantly have to replace it.

If you spend a couple extra bucks on your backpack, you probably will never have to replace it... Ever.

Personally, I'm a big fan of Osprey packs. I've had the SAME Osprey pack for **seven years** now.

You heard me right, **seven years**.

How the hell is that possible I hear you ask? Simple, Osprey packs are damn well made, they are light, comfortable, tough and crucially they have a hip-belt meaning you can trek with up to twenty kilos of gear relatively comfortably.

But best of all, Osprey packs have a lifetime warranty.

You can send your pack back to Osprey and as long as you cover postage they will fix any rips or broken zips. I have had to send my pack back twice over seven years - it gets a lot of use - and both times they have replaced entire panels with no problems.

Your pack is an investment... Make it an investment that will last forever. You can get a decent bag for under $200.

There are **four** things you need to consider when searching for your soul-pack.

LOVE AT FIRST PACK

The four things you need for the backpack of your dreams

THE RIGHT SIZE

I never recommend going over 70L, packs over this size are just too big. If you are under six foot, 40L-60L will be absolutely perfect

COMFORT

No matter the size, backpacks can get heavy and will put a strain on your back. An internal frame is 100% imperative, as is shoulder padding. A hipbelt is handy if you plan to trek with your pack.

WATER RESISTANT

Rain. Ocean. Beer. The last thing you need is your entire life's worth of stuff saturated by a cheap pint of Tsing Tao

COMPARTMENTS

Abra-Cadabra! Seriously, hidden compartments are like magic. You'll develop your own system of where everything goes, but the more options the better - keep an eye out for packs with plenty of storage options.

www.TheBrokeBackpacker.com

I prefer to travel with one medium sized pack that can be used for trekking (i.e. it has a hipbelt!) and another daypack for my camera, laptop and valuables so I can keep them close to hand on bus or train journeys.

I've written about how to pick the best backpack for your travels a lot on the blog. If you are looking for a pack specifically for hiking, check out this post:

www.thebrokebackpacker.com/best-backpacks-for-hiking

If you simply want to choose the best allrounder pack for travel, start here:

www.thebrokebackpacker.com/best-travel-backpack

Hitching and Camping Gear

If you are down to camp and hitch, you have to accept that you'll have a bit more stuff than the average backpacker and your packing strategy will greatly differ from someone who can always afford to splash out on a room.

Make a decision on whether or not you plan to hitch regularly, if you do then you will need to take a tent so that you have greater flexibility and don't get caught out with nowhere to sleep. If you are travelling on a really tight budget, you should definitely take a tent with you as it will save you a boatload of money.

Now if you **are** hitching and camping, there's a few things you'll need…

- A sharpie is probably the most important tool for any successful hitchhiking expedition. Surprisingly, finding cardboard to write on is never a challenge. Keep few good pens in your bag.

- A head torch so you can see and so cars can see if you if you end up walking in dark.
- Pocket Rocket stove - not essential but if you're doing a lot of camping and hitchhiking, it can be very helpful.
- Weather-relevant clothing: If it's cold, you will need cold weather gear… or you risk dying.
- Tent, roll mat – it's possible to get by with just these for a night's sleep. Don't get me wrong, I've slept both rough and with just a tent (no roll mat) before but if you're taking a tent it's well worth taking the roll mat. You CAN get by without a sleeping bag if it's not too cold but without a roll mat you'll be in for a very uncomfortable night's sleep.

Packing Lists

One of the most common questions I get from folks about to hit the road on a round the world trip is *"what gear should I take backpacking?'*.

I have changed and adapted my backpacking packing list over nine years of travel.

We'll start with the necessities, then talk about what you might need depending on the type of trip you are taking.

I want to keep this concise and light. If you are looking for more information on specific products or want to do a bit more research, head to The Broke Backpacker. On the site I go into a lot more details about tents, cameras, backpacks and all that jazz.

Essentials Checklist

The stuff that you absolutely 100% need.

- **Backpack:** You can't be a backpacker without a backpack! I suggest picking a backpack in the fifty to seventy liters range. Picking the right travel backpack is very important; you are, after all, going to be pretty much living out of your pack

- **Daypack (10-20 liters):** A very worthwhile investment is a decent daypack – Berghaus, Osprey and Lowe Pro make the best daypacks.

- **Trekking trainers:** Don't go travelling around the world without some decent shoes! I personally swear by North Face Hedgehogs and have been wearing them for nearly a decade.

- **Compression packing cubes:** The ultimate backpacker secret weapon is keeping your stuff organised. Be sure to get a mesh laundry bag to keep your dirty laundry in, it'll stink otherwise.

- **Dry bag:** Well worth having to keep your electronics in… Mine has saved my gear on more than one occasion. A five litre dry-bag is normally big enough.

- **Hanging toiletry bag:** Hand's down the easiest way to keep all your toiletries and meds in one place. I never really feel like I've moved into a place until I hang it up…

- **World Travel Adapter:** It's worth splashing out a bit here and getting one that can charge a laptop and two USB devices at once, I have been using my Skross Travel Adapter for years.

- **Some clothes:** Underwear x 5, T-shirts x 3, trousers x

2, fleece x 1, baselayer x 1 (more on clothes later).

You can get away with just the above and hell, it's worth considering - the less you have, the easier it'll be to pack up on the road! Still, there are plenty more useful things you can take travelling and some of the below should be considered. I choose what to travel with depending on where I am going and what the climate will be like.

Clothing checklist

The one thing that people overpack (cough; ladies) is clothing. Keep your clothing to a minimum! You'll only need a few pairs of outfits and as mentioned, if you need anything else you can always pick it up while on the road.

- **Technical sandals:** If you're going to be spending a lot of time trekking in the jungle, hanging out on the beach or sailing then it's worth bringing a pair of good quality technical sandals; Teva and Merrel make the best sandals.

- **Flip Flops:** Definitely worth packing no matter where you are going (you'll need these for hostel showers).

- **Sunhat:** If you're heading to the scorched plains of Backpackistan, you need to keep your head covered. My Barmah bush-hat has accompanied me on many adventures.

- **Buff:** One of my favourite travel accessories, I wear a buff on my wrist at all times; it's great for keeping the sun off or covering your mouth and nose to keep dust out. I also use it as an eye mask on long haul transport and in dorm rooms.

- **Underwear**: It can be surprisingly hard to find underwear that fits in Asia... Pack 4-5 pairs.

- **Thin hiking trousers**: Craghoppers make the best stuff and their Nosquito range is impregnated with mosquito repellant.

- **Long sleeved mosquito repellent shirt**: A life saver when trekking or hanging out in tropical climates. Again – check out Craghoppers.

- **T-shirts / Tank tops** x 4: Easy to find on the road if you need replacements.

- **Base layer**: Crucial for keeping warm, I swear by my Helley Hansen.

- **Lightweight technical fleece**: Essential when you're on buses or trains that have the AC turned to 'freezing'.

- **Evening wear** for going out: Again, I tend to stick to Craghoppers; they have some smart shirts which are also fairly practical.

- **Indestructible sunglasses**: I have probably destroyed over one hundred pairs of sunglasses... For a backpacking adventure, it's worth investing in a decent pair of sunnies and I recommend Sungod; these are specifically built for travellers and are pretty much impossible to break.

Technology Checklist

- **Camera** – Unless you are lucky enough to already own a DSLR, you probably won't end up taking one travelling with you. Camera phones are more than adequate so certainly don't worry about buying a camera just for travelling. If you do want to invest in a new camera but don't want to buy a DSLR, a Lumix is a good place to start – they offer great bang for your buck, good photo quality and are easy to use.

- **Laptop:** You do not need a laptop to travel the world. For many years, I travelled without a laptop or a phone and it was an awesome experience. Having tech on your adventure will definitely carry some disadvantages, despite your best intentions it will be harder to disconnect from the Matrix. If you plan on eventually making money online whilst travelling, you will definitely need a laptop and it's a solid investment - check out this post for a ton of practical info on choosing a travel friendly laptop - www.thebrokebackpacker.com/best-travel-laptop-for-digital-nomads - but do remember, for the casual backpacker – a laptop is not a must-have item.

- **USB flash drive**: Endlessly helpful.

- **USB card reader**: Essential if you're into your photography.

- **Smartphone**: Most backpackers these days have a phone.

- **Portable battery**: Extremely useful for keeping your phone and camera charged whilst adventuring. I travel with two as I'm often trekking and away from power.

- **GoPro Hero 5**: If you want an action cam, this is the one to go for…

Adventure Checklist

Going trekking in Nepal? Safari-ing in Africa? Hiking the Andes? Camping in the Amazon? This list is for you.

- **Head-torch**: Super useful for caving, hiking and bathroom trips when the power's gone out. I never travel without a head-torch; it's saved my life multiple times.

- **Mosquito net**: If you do need a mosquito net, pick a box-shaped net (four hanging points) – it is significantly more spacious and comfortable to sleep under than a pyramid-shaped net (one hanging point).

- **Cable ties**: Always worth packing a couple, especially if you're off on a motorbiking adventure.

- **Carabiners**: I always attach two or three of these to my pack, they are endlessly helpful.

- **Sleeping bag liner**: Useful when the sheets are not so clean or you want to sleep under a blanket but it's damn hot.

- **Small sewing kit**: Fix your own clothes and you'll save some money.

- **Combination padlock**: I used to frequently lose my room keys when staying in hostels, these days I just lock my room with my own padlock, problem solved.

- **Pens and notebook**: Journaling isn't dead, damn it!

Hiking Gear Checklist

If you're planning an epic expedition and will be away from civilization, it does make sense to invest in some of this.

- **Warm gear**: If you're heading into the mountains, pick up a pair of **water-resistant gloves**, a **hat with ear-flaps** and a down jacket; I've been using my **RAB Neutrino** for years and it was a great investment.

- **Water bottle**: Hydration is pretty damn important whilst trekking, I recommend a **Nalgene** as it's wide enough to clean easily.

- **UV Steripen**: The best option for purifying water.

- **Water purification tabs**: A much cheaper option for purifying water.

- **Multi-tool**: I've been using my ultra lightweight **Leatherman Skeletool** for years, it's the perfect companion for any backpacking adventure.

- **Portable stove**: I have a **pocket-rocket** which serves me well.

- **Tent**: If you're camping, you'll need a tent... **Vango** make some of the best value quality tents on the market and **MSR** make the best tents in the world. Check out this article for a comparison of some of the best tents around – www.thebrokebackpacker.com/best-backpacking-tent
- **Roll-mat and sleeping bag: Thermarest** makes some very good, albeit, expensive stuff.
- A proper hiking backpack.

Toiletries Checklist

- **Toothbrush and toothpaste**
- **Shower gel**
- **Cotton buds**
- **Pack of tissues**
- **Decent sunscreen** (often expensive to buy abroad)
- **Deodorant**
- **Nail clipper**
- **Moisturiser** (for sunburn)
- **Razor with replacement blades**
- **Shaving gel**
- **Earplugs**
- **Condoms**
- **Girly stuff** (if applicable!)
- **Microfibre travel towel** – significantly better than using scummy hostel towels.

Medical Checklist

It's always worth packing a first aid kit. On my travels I've been hospitalised three times, been in a couple of motorbike accidents and had more hangovers than I can count. My first aid kit saved my ass on more than one occasion…

I recommend picking up a **pre-assembled first-aid kit** and then pimping it out with all of the below.

- **Personal medicines such as inhalers**
- **Paracetamol, ibuprofen and aspirin**
- **Disinfectant spray**
- **Disinfectant wipes**
- **Mosquito repellent** (at least 40% deet)
- **Antihistamines**
- **Bandages and gauze**
- **Plasters in various sizes**
- **Steri-strips**
- **Throat lozenges**
- **Condoms**
- **Ciprofloxacin** (the best thing to take for traveler's diarrhoea)
- **Malaria pills** if applicable

Documents Checklist

It helps to be organised before you hit the road; I travel with all of the below in a plastic wallet, it may sound nerdy but when you're at a politically charged border crossing you will get across a lot faster if you are organised.

- **Flight, train and bus tickets**

- **Address of your first hostel** (even if it's fake).
- **Valid passport**
- **Laminated copy of your passport**
- **Debit cards** x 2
- **Credit card**
- **Dollars or Euros**
- **RFID Blocking Money Belt**
- **Some one dollar bills for tips**
- **Driver's license**
- **Student ID**
- **Half a dozen passport photos for visas on arrival** (you normally need two per visa).
- **Insurance information**, home contact details, health information as part of a laminated card.

Gear Summary

Everyone has the capacity to overpack, especially if you are planning on some hiking and adventuring. Travel light, if you can, there are numerous advantages. Remember that you can often pick up hiking gear on the road so there's no point in carrying too much specialist gear around if you won't get to use it for several months. Plan your adventures and pack accordingly.

Travel Insurance

If you recall, I mentioned travel insurance as one of the top five things you absolutely NEED while travelling the world.

"But Will - you're The Broke Backpacker! Insurance? I thought you were more hardcore than that!"

Well trust me, if you're hitting the road, you can't afford **not** to get travel insurance.

I've had to claim on my insurance a total of four times - once for upwards of $20,000 to cover medical bills - and I always travel with insurance. Insurance gives you the freedom to enjoy your trip with the knowledge that if something goes wrong, you are covered.

If you do hit the road long-term, it's not a case of if something goes wrong - it's **when**. Just get the damn insurance.

Essential Coverage

On any good backpacker travel insurance policy, all of the below should be included, if something is missing from your policy then consider looking for a different provider. Your backpacking insurance policy should…

- Cover most countries in the world.
- Cover for lost, stolen or damaged luggage, possessions, documents etc
- The option to increase cover of high-value items e.g. a laptop
- Helpline: A 24-hour emergency helpline.
- At least £1 million personal liability insurance in case you injure a person or cause damage to their property.
- A minimum of £1 million of medical cover.
- Repatriation to your home country in the case of

serious illness or injury – check the small print, occasionally the repatriation will only take you so far.

- A minimum of £1000 cancellation / curtailment cover so that you can get home fast if there is an emergency such as a death in the family.
- Cover for any legal expenses you may need.
- Extendibility: If you decide to travel for longer than originally planned you want to be able to extend your policy easily.

Things to Consider Before Buying Backpacker Insurance

- **Small print:** Many travel insurance policies will not cover you if you are injured whilst doing any kind of 'high adrenaline' activity so it is crucial you read your policy and understand it. Sometimes even hill walking is classified as 'high adrenaline'. For an extra premium you can usually add activities to your policy, think about what you will be doing and add accordingly. If you are trekking make sure your policy will cover rescue at your elevation as if you are not covered you may have to pay for the rescue helicopter yourself.

- **Alcohol and drugs:** Most travel insurance policies will not cover you if you were under the influence of alcohol and drugs at the time of an accident. Try to avoid getting breathalysed if you get injured whilst drunk.

- **Valuables & electronics insurance:** Almost all cheap backpacker insurance policies will have very high excesses and fixed limits on the amount you can claim on personal belongings. Ideally, you should pay a bit more to properly insure your valuables. Whether you choose to insure your gear is up to you; certainly your overall policy will cost more if you do. You may be better off just keeping a bloody good eye on your valuables and not paying the extra money to insure them.

How to Make a Claim on Your Travel Insurance Policy

If you need to make a claim, get all your documents in order early on. This is the best piece of advice I can give you.

If you have been robbed, you will need a police report… In general, getting a police report tends to vastly speed up getting payment out of an insurance company.

Keeping receipts of all the valuables you take travelling is another really good idea – the insurance company will want to see that you actually bought the items in the first place before they pay out.

You need to be patient when it comes to actually getting paid as even the best insurance companies sometimes drag their feet. If the first offer that the travel insurance company makes you is ridiculously low then dispute it – the second offer is usually a lot better.

Cost of Travel Insurance

Travel insurance comes in all different policies, coverage,

shapes, sizes and most importantly... prices!

You are more than welcome to take out more expensive policies - but I never do.

Good standard travel insurance usually averages out to be a dollar a day.

One buck every day to make sure that if something *terrible* happens, you're good to go. It's worth it.

Which Travel Insurance Company to Pick

As much of a rebel as I like to be, I'm going to go **with** the grain on this one.

World Nomads (see URL in back of book) is largely considered to be the best travel insurance provider out there.

By best I don't mean cheapest. By best I mean, most likely to actually pay you if they owe you.

World Nomads is the only insurance provider I know of that lets you buy travel insurance *after* leaving your home country.

In general, insurance companies are bastards, World Nomads are better than most and have always paid out when I've claimed.

They have a wide range of policies, many of which are high in coverage and fairly affordable – around a dollar a day.

If you are looking for the absolute cheapest insurance, check out *insure and go*. They are as cheap as it gets, but remember amigos, you always get what you pay for.

In general, insuring your valuables and electronics is the most expensive part of any insurance policy as the majority of insurance claims are for stolen cameras, laptops and phones. I personally have a medical and health insurance policy with World Nomads and then a separate insurance policy for my gear with Gadget Cover - I haven't tried to claim from Gadget Cover before so I don't know how good they are.

Find out more about travel insurance policies on the site: www.thebrokebackpacker.com/cheap-backpacker-insurance

Chapter Summary

There's a lot of stuff you *can* bring on your travels but only a handful of things you *need* to bring. Remember that travelling light is the key, and you can pick up anything else that you might need whilst on the road.

- Travel as light as you can but pack things which are hard to buy outside of your home country.
- Spend proper money on your backpack and camping gear. These are the two things that need a proper investment – if you decide to buy camping gear that is. By biting the bullet and putting in the money, you will save yourself years of future headaches.
- Buy the God-damn insurance.
- Do some research and compare policies to figure out which travel insurance is best for you.

Chapter Seven
Staying Safe on the Road

At the end of the day, staying safe on the road is pretty simple. Are there dangers in the world? Certainly. Are some areas of the world a little dodgier than others? Absolutely.

But I promise you - the world is a much safer place than you have been led to believe.

This is because our view of the world has a tendency to be shaped by the media… and the media are no longer reliable. #fakenews

This is because many news agencies have abandoned dignity and integrity in journalism and replaced it with sensationalism, click bait titles and a negative perspective on the world.

Negativity sells. Positivity doesn't. Which article are you going to click on?

Generous Indian woman pays cab fare for struggling neighbor

Or.

Breaking News! Polish man high on bath salts eats his own face before strangling an innocent puppy to death!

You and everyone else on this earth is going innocent-puppy-strangling 99 times out of 100. So don't just blame the dirty clickbait sensationalistic media, because at the end of the day we all need to change our attitudes and stop clicking on bullshit.

Whilst once in a million years a Polish man high on bath salts may strangle an innocent puppy to death…. Every day millions of people are doing the right thing - paying for stranger's cabs, helping their neighbors, paying it forward and just smiling, being decent people.

This is the way the world *really* works.

So now that we've established we are all to blame, let's right our wrongs by fixing this inaccurate negative perception of the world by admitting…

The world is **not** out to get you!

It just isn't. People have their own stuff in their own lives to worry about.

If you should be worried about someone, there is one person in particular you should spend time and attention ensuring is on the right track.

You.

You are your own worst enemy, and this is exponentially true as a backpacker. Ultimately any kind of trouble you get into abroad is probably going to be your fault. The best piece of advice I can give you is to constantly be aware that backpackers are some of the most beautiful idiots you will ever meet.

Sure, taking mushrooms and dancing till dawn on a clifftop may be fun… but it *is* dangerous.

I'm not saying you shouldn't do it but you need to weigh up the risks. Riding a motorbike without any training is exhilarating but what if you crash? If someone's idea for a 'great time' sounds stupid, it probably is.

Real Dangers to Backpackers

Out of all of the dangers that backpackers and world travelers face… there is one thing that, above all, claims many backpackers each year.

This thing doesn't always necessarily claim the *lives* of backpackers, but it claims other things…. Wallets, passports, virginity, the occasional eyeball and more often than not - personal dignity.

I'm talking about the number one danger while backpacking the world - alcohol.

Alcohol

I'll make this brief, I'm not here to be you mum and tell you alcohol can be dangerous, but let's be honest, alcohol can be really dangerous.

And it's not the booze itself, it's the liquid induced courage that comes from the booze and the decisions that we then choose to make with those six shots of tequila sprinting through our blood like a million Usain Bolts jacked up on cocaine.

It's what we do *after* drinking the booze that we need to worry about. It's deciding to drive a scooter at night in Bangkok. It's getting a bit too close to the fire spinner during their grand finale. It's about saying *'Sure ladies, I'll come inside that shady looking brothel! Me love you long time too!'*. It's when you decide to go for the midnight dip in the ocean. It's about trying to score drugs off someone shady at 2 am and getting robbed before you know what's happening.

These are situations you might not have normally found

yourself in, but alcohol can really give us quite the nudge, can't it?

So just know that many of the bad situations travellers get themselves in usually involves the consumption of a bit too much alcohol.

So be smart, and an *extra* word of warning to the ladies. Drink and be merry! **But be aware.**

Drugs

I smoked my first joint whilst backpacking in India. I was nineteen and soaking in some truly stunning mountain views. Unsure of what to expect, I had joined a small smoking circle of travellers and was curious to see what all the fuss was about. The first hit of THC hit me like a soft pillow to the face. I smiled, lay down and watched the clouds go by…

I'll come clean right now, I've experimented with a lot of drugs over the years. I've had some meaningful experiences, some potent revelations and some unforgettable evenings as a result of this. These have not always been good experiences and it's important to treat substances with respect.

Whilst I do **not** recommend that every budding psychonaut down a mushroom shake, I do think it's important to arm backpackers with the information they need to make an informed decision and to practice safe drug use – yep, there is such a thing.

Marijuana

This is usually the most popular drug available to backpackers as it is cheap and relatively easy to find. Sharing a joint whilst relaxing with mates or enjoying a cheeky smoke whilst overlooking the mountains of Pakistan is a great way to end the day.

Slowly but surely, marijuana is becoming legalised in more and more parts of the world and hopefully one day it will be decriminalized everywhere – **until that happens though, you really don't want to get caught smoking weed whilst travelling…**

Some countries still have very strict laws surrounding all drugs, including weed, and there are plenty of scams out there – especially in backpacker hubs like Goa; be careful who you buy from. In particular, Indonesia's drug laws are especially strict so you need to watch yourself no matter where you are…

Magic Mushrooms

The most widely available psychedelic on the backpacker circuit, shrooms can be found in many party hubs and are especially easy to find in Laos and Thailand. Most of the time, shrooms are blended up into a not-so-tasty mushroom shake. Banana or mango is a good choice of mixer.

I've taken mushroom shakes a few times in the past, personally I prefer other psychedelics. If you are going to try a mushroom shake (keep an eye out for happy shakes and happy pizzas!) be sure not to overdo it and that you are around people you are comfortable with.

Ecstasy

MDMA (the active ingredient in ecstasy) is the drug of choice for many travellers. The problem with ecstasy pills is that it's impossible to know how much MDMA they actually contain and whether or not the pills have been cut with something else, usually they have and usually it's speed.

In general, you get what you pay for so beware of super cheap drugs whilst travelling. Be seriously careful with dosage when taking ecstasy and avoid mixing with alcohol – the results can be pretty horrendous.

Cocaine

You'll find cocaine when travelling to South America, especially Colombia or Bolivia. Coke is a great party drug and, in South America, is seriously cheap. It is however seriously addictive and kicking the habit is horrible – expect cold sweats, nightmares and irrational thoughts. If you plan on doing cocaine whilst travelling in South America, try to keep a lid on it and not to do it too often.

LSD

LSD, or Acid, is a powerful psychedelic which needs to be treated with real respect. I do not recommend trying LSD for the first time at a festival or large event – LSD is better used for spiritual exploration rather than as a party drug, in my opinion.

Drugs on the road

Many first-time travellers are also first-time drug users. I know plenty of backpackers who smoked their first joint, sipped their first mushroom shake or took their first pill whilst letting their hair down in the crazed party meccas of South East Asia. Some backpackers are interested in trying drugs simply because they are there, others are looking for something a little bit deeper. Whilst I don't want to flat out condone drug use I am extremely reluctant to condemn it. Drugs are, to some, tools and they have been around for thousands of years.

Like any tool, certain drugs can only be used for certain tasks. Much like a workman attempting to hammer in nails with a saw, you can get into real trouble if you use the wrong drug under the wrong circumstances. And like a kid attempting to operate a jackhammer, you can find yourself in danger if you don't know what you're doing.

There is a compelling amount of evidence out there to suggest that psychedelics have important therapeutic applications. Recently, I met a wandering nomad who had suffered a life changing injury when he was younger. He told me that it was only when he began experimenting with psychedelics that he was finally able to put everything into perspective, let go of some negative feelings and move on. For some, discovering psychedelics can be a life changing moment.

On the other hand, if you have a history of mental illness within your family, it's best to give drugs a miss. Marijuana, for example, has been linked to schizophrenia by some studies. At the end of the day – the most important thing to remember with drugs is to partake in moderation.

As much as I like smoking weed, I find myself slipping into lazy habits when I smoke too much – in the same way that drinking too much alcohol can get in the way of your everyday life, over the top drug use is not a good thing. I recommend steering clear of Ketamine and Opiates.

So if you *are* planning on experimenting with drugs on your travels, it's important to play it safe and keep it moderate. Here's some extra tips for experimenting with drugs...

Practising Safe Drug Use

• **Place**: The most important part of any drug experience is the setting. You need to feel comfortable, you don't want to feel overwhelmed by what's going on around you.

• **People**: Make sure you trust the people you are with, people can act differently to what you are used to when they are stoned – in the same way that your best mate can be a total idiot when he's pissed. Ideally, you want to be with a few friends you know well

• **Dosage**: Don't overdo it, if you're trying a new substance for the very first time then don't go crazy, pace it out.

• **Identify Risks**: Be aware of the risks, when you are on drugs, or drunk for that matter, your ability to recognise risks can be impaired. Keep away from water (don't go swimming) and traffic.

• **Alcohol**: Do not drink alcohol and mix drugs, the results can be unpleasant (or deadly).

• **Don't drive**: The biggest cause of death and injury to backpackers is still motorbike accidents... the chances of something going wrong dramatically increases when you are drunk or on drugs and decide to try and drive home. Just don't do it.

• **Stay hydrated**: Seriously, drink plenty of water.

When it comes to drug use on the backpacker circuit, there's no ignoring it, it is out there and it won't be going away anytime soon. For many backpackers, travelling is all about trying new experiences and drugs are a small part of that.

Do your research before you make an informed decision

and be aware that there is a huge amount of misinformation floating around the internet.

Travel far, love often and, as always, only experiment with drugs if you truly want to. Never feel pressured to get involved in something which doesn't interest you – whether it's a cheeky smoke in India, a mushroom shake in Thailand or anything else at all.

Some backpackers prefer to watch a sunset with a cold beer in one hand, others prefer a joint. Each to their own, live and let live and wherever you may be on the road; enjoy the journey.

Disclaimer: Drugs are illegal and can get you in sticky situations. I don't condone drug use of any sort. If you intend to consume, please be safe. This chapter is not intended to persuade, but rather to inform.

Traffic / Motorbikes

Intoxicants aside, there are still a handful of things to keep an eye out for - cars and motorbikes being one of them!

One of the leading causes of death / injury to travellers is traffic.

The most common is through the backpackers greatest friend / enemy - the motorbike!

Motorbikes, scooters, mopeds – whatever, these are a deadly good time.

Motorbikes are a cheap and convenient way to get around. The majority of drivers in developing nations use some kind of motorbike. As a traveller they are efficient and they don't cost much to rent or even buy... Plus, it's damn fun driving around.

But they can be deadly. One slip, one mishap by you (or another driver!) and you are at the mercy of velocity and gravity.

So my first tidbit of advice is this - if you have no experience riding a motorbike, don't try it in a city or built up area. It's just not worth it. The flow of automobiles in developing nations resembles anarchy and while you might get a feel for it, learning in a city is not recommended.

Now, if you feel confident in your ability to operate a motorbike, or just think *'Hey Will, go fuck yourself, I'm gonna do it anyways!"*, then please, heed this advice…

1. Wear a helmet
2. Wear good shoes

Yes, I know. A helmet? So boring. So lame! It's not what you imagined. Motorbiking through The Philippines, hair dancing in the wind… a helmet screws all that up!

Wearing a helmet could save your life. It saved mine. Twice.

I have been involved in two accidents with motorbikes whilst wearing a helmet, once in India and once in Vietnam resulting in various exciting injuries.

On **BOTH** occasions my helmet saved my life. In Vietnam the bike flipped, I went flying and landed with a bump, the bike then hit me in the head. I had a hell of a headache but I survived.

More recently, I was involved in an accident in Thailand. I had two chicks on the back of my bike and had given them both of the helmets. I ended up with a large open wound above my eye and had to get nine stitches. The girls were both fine, if I had been wearing a helmet then I would have been fine too.

So please - put a helmet on your head, buckle it, and be at

ease as you cruise and navigate the narrow streets of Backpackistan.

As for the shoes? Protect your feet. If an accident occurs, your cardboard flip flops won't offer you any protection. Wearing shoes literally saved my feet. When I crashed, my shoes were shredded but they saved my feet. Save your feet damn it!

Do not operate any vehicle while under the influence of any intoxicant, it's just a bad idea.

Water

Drink it, but don't swim in it when you're drunk.

Along with traffic accidents, death by drowning is common in the travelling world.

Sometimes freak accidents happen where people are sober and drown. But it's usually the late night ocean dip after three Thai buckets mixed with two Long Island Iced Teas you need to be careful of.

Pools, rivers, oceans, lakes, baths, hot tubs - just be wary of water (especially when you've been drinking).

Precautions Against Theft

There are two main steps to take precautions against theft.

1. Make your stuff less accessible to be stolen
2. Ensure you have back-ups in case your stuff does get stolen

Both of these are important. You can take every precaution in the book, but at the end of the day there are situations where there will be little you can do so it's important to plan for the worst case scenario.

Hide Your Gear (precautions to avoid theft)

Most of this is straightforward. As we've mentioned, while most of humanity is cool, there's a handful of twats out there, and they might be eyeing up your stuff.

1. **Always lock up your stuff**. If you are in a hostel, put your bag in the provided lockers. It takes three extra seconds and could mean the difference between having the time of your life and getting your backpack stolen.

2. **Hostel precautions** - If you are staying in hostels, you can ask them to keep your bag behind the front desk. This is a good way to feel the extra bit of confidence if you are headed out for an entire day

3. **Use locks!** Bring your own padlock (hostels might provide lockers, but not locks) and more importantly, bring padlocks for your bag!! They must be small locks that can fit lock the zippers. This simple action can be a major deterrence for someone's sticky fingers looking to make a quick move.

4. **Don't walk the streets** – Get a feel for the local area by asking the staff at your hostel. In some countries, like Venezuela, walking around after dark is a really bad move and you will quickly get mugged. This is not the case in most countries but it is like this in a few so do your research and avoid being caught out.

5. **Hide your money** – Money is the most steal-able thing you are carrying around. I always have a small amount of money in a wallet which I can give away if somebody mugs me

with a knife. The rest of my money is hidden away in several different locations. I've experimented with loads of different means of hiding money but using a specially made security belt, link on the back page, is by far the best bet.

6. **Do not leave your gear unattended unless it's locked up** – Just don't do it.

Backup Plans (in case shit hits the fan)

You could be the safest dude on the planet, having taken every precaution known to independent travelers everywhere… but you still might get unlucky. Here's how you can plan in advance to tackle disaster…

1. **Back up documents:** You should have photocopies of your passport, bank cards and insurance policy somewhere safe – these days, the best bet is to hold them in a cloud storage service like Dropbox. I also strongly recommend backing up your photos and moves to Dropbox regularly so that if your memory card is lost or damaged, you haven't lost all of your photos. I've covered this extensively on the site – www.thebrokebackpacker.com/top-digital-backup-and-security-tips

2. **Back up money in two places.** While in Venezuela; I carried $200 hidden in a fold in my specially designed belt (see URL in back of book), as well as more dollars concealed between two laminated photographs (which had to be cut open) in my 'photo book' from home. Craghoppers makes some good clothing with hidden security pockets. Never have all of your money, or all of your debit cards, in one place.

Travelling as a Woman

If travelling alone as a woman intimidates you, don't let it.

Because believe it or not, there are literally tens of thousands of women solo backpacking the world right now.

I know this because I've met thousands of them myself.

These days I'd say I run into nearly just as many solo female backpackers as I do solo male backpackers. It's amazing to see so many women feeling empowered and independent, and it's exponentially inspiring more women to do the same.

But that doesn't mean there aren't dangers for women. A true adventure is one which follows a road less travelled and that can sometimes mean uncertainty, risk and danger. I don't mind admitting that there have been times out on the road when I have been somewhat afraid and it is often said that travelling is far scarier and more dangerous for women. Perhaps once that was true, perhaps it is still true, all I know is that I am meeting more and more kick ass female solo travellers.

I've got some personal tips for chicks, but I've also spoke to some of the most awesome female travellers I know. This is a list of some of their best travel tips for chicks. *(Gentlemen, check this out too, there's some good general advice in here).*

- **Trust your gut.** It's the most powerful radar you possess. Whatever your head says, let your gut have the final say. If you feel something isn't right, just walk away and leave, but also...

- **Don't give into fear.** Travelling solo is a way to become a more independent, braver, adventurous and educated woman. If you think you can't do something, at least give yourself the chance to try. Nine times out of ten, you will achieve what you thought you couldn't and be amazed at your own capabilities.

• **Learn to defend yourself.** The world is safe but there are still a handful of people who aren't as nice as you. Know how to handle yourself if it comes to the crunch (more on this in a bit)

• If you're feeling unsure about a situation **attach yourself to a family or woman nearby**.

• **Don't be scared to make noise.** If someone isn't treating you right, make a scene. It will show how strong you are and will probably scare them off!

• **Leave your itinerary with someone you trust.** No matter what your age, or how independent you are, never underestimate the importance of letting people know where you are/will be. Post regular updates on social media to let people know back home you're safe.

• **Don't get blind drunk.** If you're travelling alone, especially as a female, getting wasted abroad can be a recipe for disaster. You're in a foreign country, potentially with little knowledge of the local language, customs and laws, with people you may have only just met. Alcohol dulls your senses and makes you vulnerable.

• **Try your best to blend in.** Avoid wearing flashy jewelry or anything that draws attention to yourself. The more you stand out, the more vulnerable you are to crime.

A special thanks to Teacake Travels, Castaway with Crystal, Lucy Smiles Away, Journalist on the Run, Coffee with a Slice of Life, and Mapping Megan for these awesome tips for travelling chicks!

When to Run and When to Fight

If you are in a situation where you feel endangered, running is often the safest bet. It will attract attention, cause a scene, and most importantly - get you the heck out of Dodge. Plus, the adrenaline pumping through your veins will also give you superhuman speeds, enabling you to outrun any muggers.

If there is a weapon involved, drop you shit, and BOOK IT.

I say drop your shit for two reasons. 1. It'll lighten your load, enabling you to hit superhuman speeds and 2. You'll increase the chances of being left alone.

The reason muggers steal is not for pleasure, but for your stuff. If you drop your wallet and hit 25 mph heading towards people while yelling 'HELP!', do you think for a split second the mugger is going to follow you?

Hell no.

And while you might lose your goods (money, passport, weed, etc) it's preferable to getting stabbed in the neck with a rusty dagger.

This again is why we have travel insurance kids!

The only times you should fight is if you literally have no other choice. Saying that, this is also the reason that I carry a wallet which I can afford to lose. This wallet has about $10 in it and no debit cards. If I'm in a dodgy situation, I know I can hand it over without losing anything that I desperately need. My passport, and the bulk of my money, is always well hidden.

How to Defend Yourself

Now, while the world as a whole isn't out to get you, bad people happen, and if they do decide to 'get you', it's best to be as prepared as possible.

If you decide you need to defend yourself and you can't run - strike fast, strike hard and strike first. I emphasize this again – strike first. You can usually gain the upper hand just by striking first. Go for the eyes, throat or balls. A chop or punch to the throat will buy you a good ten seconds to get away from your attacker.

Going for the balls is another obvious option but be careful with kicking, if your attacker has any training they may catch your leg and flip you onto the ground thus making your situation worse.

Strike fast, strike hard, strike first... but only when you have to.

Then run.

Also, if you've got some time before setting off for your trip and are nervous about self defense, take up a few classes! Most towns in the world have a boxing, Karate, Muay Thai or MMA gym.

You only need to get down a move or two to become someone who can actually defend themselves in certain situations. A mere few months of technical training will literally put you above 95% of the human population.

And that's the point. Most thieves and muggers are drug addicts or poor and hungry. They are not UFC fighters. They are not trained. They are just desperate and often they are not even bad people, they are just down on their luck. Even a small bit of training will put you miles in front of the typical mugger.

So while my best piece of advice is to run, if you are nervous about personal safety and want to prepare yourself *just in case* - take a few classes! Learn the ropes, enhance your coordination, get the technique down and master a few signature moves. It'll equate to an enormous increase in confidence while travelling.

What to Do if You're Mugged (or worse)

Go to the police station and file a report. While there are no guarantees, having a police report will encourage your insurer to pay up prompto! Depending on your situation, find another backpacker and explain what's going on – we are all one tribe and usually other backpackers will help you.

Digital Security and Backups

You'll likely have some electronics with you, so it's good to keep them secure and backed up. I won't dive too deep into this, but there's two ways to keep your cherished memories protected.

1. Hard drive - You can store all of your photos and videos on an external hard drive. Doing so ensures that your stuff is backed up and keeps space clear on your computer. This is recommended for working or aspiring Digital Nomads. The only issue with hard drives is they are not failproof.

2. Backing up your data through cloud storage is a great idea. Personally I use Crashplan, so if I lose my laptop I can

download the entire contents of my old laptop to a new one. Having this will costs just $5 a month but is well worth it if you are a digital nomad and run your life from your laptop...

The World is Safe

Bad shit can happen, but you'll have clear control over the situations you put yourself in. If you are smart and diligent, there's a 99.9% chance nothing bad will ever happen to you.

And if you are in a serious situation, you now know what to do – strike hard, strike fast, strike first – and then get out of there. It's not a cowardly move, it's the smart move.

Chapter Summary

While the world is mostly safe, you've got to be smart, follow these guidelines to keep yourself safe...

- Do not attempt to learn how to drive a motorbike in areas with crazy traffic. If you want to learn, do so in a closed safe area - not the heart of Bangkok.
- Never operate a motor vehicle while drunk or high. Maybe back home you could have a few beers and be fine, but traffic in other parts of the world is different and even if you are a great driver, that doesn't mean that everybody else on the road is. Walk or grab the bus or a cab. Doing so could save your life.
- Always wear a helmet and shoes when on a motorbike.

If you do get into an accident, this will double your chances of survival and avoiding nasty injuries. And always ensure that your helmet is secured! (It won't do a bloody thing if it's not strapped up properly).

- Be smart when swimming. We all like to have a couple of beers in the pool, but outside of traffic, drowning is the leading (non-natural) cause of death for travellers. Have a swim in the pool after a few beers. Don't go skinny dipping in the Indian Ocean off your face at three in the morning.

- Theft can happen, but the best ways to avoid it are to keep a tight head and be aware. If you have to fight, go for the eyes, throat and balls. Carry a dummy wallet that you can surrender.

- Most people in the world are decent human beings, don't be misled by some of the shitty click-bait media that's doing the rounds at the moment. The world is an awesome place, filled with awesome people.

Chapter Eight
Health is Wealth

Health is just one of those things isn't it? Like a good Wi-Fi connection or consistently getting laid. We take it for granted until it's gone.

We forget that life does not guarantee such things, and then BAM! You're a pale shell of yourself, lying on the bathroom floor, vomiting up last night's seafood, wishing sweet death would swoop in to end all the pain.

When we are sick, nothing else seems to matter. And being sick on the road can be pretty awful. Being sick at home is not so bad because we have our comfortable bed, our comfortable blankets, our comfortable bathroom with a real god-damn toilet, and maybe even an awesome mom to make us chicken noodle soup.

This will not be the case while travelling.

Frankly, getting sick in a hostel or whilst camping or Couchsurfing sucks. So let's avoid it by staying as healthy as possible. Let's get healthy!

Travel Workouts to Keep You Fit

We get sick on the road for a variety of reasons, but one of the biggest reasons is our immune system gets shot to hell.

Travel and sleeping soundly don't always go hand in

hand, and the combination can be exhausting. Exhaustion drains the immune system, leaving you more susceptible to germs and bacteria. So, let's keep our immune system strong and sexy.

The best way to accomplish this? Exercise!

I'm a fitness fanatic and always do my best to try and stay fit while travelling, I eat well, I trek often and I hit up travel WODs that don't require equipment at least three times a week.

What the heck is a WOD I hear you ask? A travel WOD is...

Workout.

Of.

The.

Day.

Whenever I am in a place long enough, I try to find a Crossfit Box (Yep, I'm part of the cult) or at least a gym with an Olympic bar so I can work on some heavy lifts. Ultimately though, the only piece of equipment you need for a travel WOD is your own body. Most of my travel WODs are made up of bodyweight exercises like press-ups, pull-ups, squats, sit-ups and burpees.

Chances are you will have more free time whilst travelling then when you are at home and ultimately getting fit and staying fit only really requires a decent time investment (45 minutes a day, four days a week is my preferred minimum) and a good attitude. Here are some of my favourite travel WODs to help you stay fit whilst travelling the world...

Five Tips For Staying Fit While Travelling

Travel Fitness Tip 1 – Soft Exercise

Staying fit becomes a lot easier if you constantly engage in soft exercise; take the stairs, have lots of sex, do some yoga.

Travel Fitness Tip 2 – Skipping

Have you got any idea just how great skipping can be for your body? There is a reason that boxers and martial artists skip religiously and I always travel with a skipping rope. Five minutes a day, especially if you are doing double unders (the rope passes under your feet twice whilst you are in the air) is incredibly good for you. I often pair skipping with my workouts when there is not room to run.

Travel Fitness Tip 3 – Avoid Sugar

Most fitness gurus now agree that sugar is the enemy… Avoid sugary drinks and beer and stick to coconut water and gin and tonic instead, it's the best way to keep those abs within sight!

Travel Fitness Tip 4 – Rock Out!

Rocks are your best friend… Whenever I find a good rock I always tend to pick it up and, depending on the situation, throw it around. It's a great way to get some impromptu strength training.

Travel Fitness Tip 5 – Go Trekking

For me, the mountains are my happy place. Whenever I

am in a country like Pakistan, India or Nepal I always make time to head off for a ten day trek into the mountains – you will come back having lost a ton of weight and will tone up quickly... Plus, mountain sunrise views are the best kind of views...

Ultimately, you are on your travels to have fun and to explore a new place – don't worry too much if your fitness slips a little bit but do try to budget four forty five minute sessions a week, at a minimum, to travel WODs that will keep you strong, healthy and attractive to the opposite sex!

Personally, fitness is a pretty big part of my life and although it does decline when I don't have access to a gym I try to make that decline as minimal as possible by staying fit on the road and utilising these travel WODs!

Five Travel WODs to Keep You Awesome

To start off my workout, I always spend about five to ten minutes stretching out and then I work in a quick 500m run or, if I'm in an enclosed space, twenty burpees to warm me up.

I usually then spend twenty minutes working on strength conditioning or a skill – like handstands. Sometimes I fill my backpack up, or try to find a good rock, and work on overhead presses, bench presses or bent over rows.

Once I'm sufficiently warm and have gotten a bit of strength training in, it's time to move on to the actual workout – I tend to pair two to three exercises together in a series of sets.

- **Travel WOD 1 – Press ups and Squats**

Perform 21, 15, 9 reps of Press ups and Squats. Finish with 10 burpees.

- **Travel WOD 2 – Burpees and Sit ups**

10 rounds of 10 Burpees and 10 Sit Ups.

- **Travel WOD 3 – Death To The Core**

Set a timer on your phone for eight rounds of 90 seconds on, 30 seconds off. Find something that you can hang from with your arms fully outstretched. Do a pull-up so that your chin is over the bar, keep your toes pointed and your abs and glutes engaged. Hold the position as long as possible, when you are close to failure, slowly let yourself down so that your arms are fully outstretched and you are hanging. Hold this position for as long as possible. When you fail, hold a plank for the remaining time. The 30 seconds is to be used as a rest.

- **Travel WOD 4 – Full Body Blast**

10 rounds: 10 press-ups, 10 squats, 10 sit-ups.

- **Travel WOD 5 – Cardio Blast**

100 Jumping Jacks, 75 Air Squats, 50 Pushups and 25 Burpees. You can make this travel WOD a bit more manageable by splitting it into five sets of 20 jumping jacks, 15 air squats, 10 pushups and 5 burpees or, if you're a traditionalist, tackle it one exercise at a time.

So there you have it, five of my favourite travel WODs to help you stay fit whilst travelling the world! Remember, you can be a broke backpacker, but you also want to be a fit backpacker. Health is wealth!

A Quick Word About Your Diet

I'm not here to lecture you. I'm not your mum. I won't make you stay at the table til you finish your peas (but peas are delicious and high in Vitamin A,C and K so you should finish your peas).

But we are talking about staying healthy, and I'd be missing out an important element if I didn't mention the importance of a proper diet.

Eating healthy can be difficult while travelling, and often it's easy to forget that your body needs fruits and veggies to operate at 100%.

It's easy to forget, I'm here to remind you not to forget. Eat well. Lay off the sugar. Lay off the fried foods. Load up on fruits and veggies every chance you get. Invest in your body, it needs to last you a lifetime.

Health Tips

There are a few other things that may seem like common sense, but you'd be surprised how many people neglect them, then wonder why they get sick! Let's go over some of the most important ones.

Stay away from the water!

So important. If you're travelling in America or France... sure, drink the tap water. It's delicious.

But when you are travelling broke in developing nations, do yourself a favor and steer clear.

It's the water that screws you up. It's carrying a ton of parasites and bacteria that you are simply not used to.

You can shower in it, you can wash your hands with it, but please for the love of god, don't put it anywhere near your mouth.

And that includes brushing your teeth! I've met many travellers who know not to *drink* the tap water, but then they brush their teeth and gargle with the same exact tap water.

I know it's less likely to get you sick from brushing, but it's still in your mouth, it can still get to your stomach. Just do yourself a favor and use some bottled water or sterilise water yourself.

Although it can be tough, avoid water offered to you by local Couchsurfing hosts, unless it's bottled or treated it will make you sick.

Water rant over.

Clean Hands = Happy Traveler

Make sure to keep your hands clean. You are going to be interacting with travellers on buses, in hostels, and everywhere in between. Not to go all hypochondriac, but it can be kind of a cesspool.

Wash your hands. A great hack is to bring alcohol gel everywhere with you. Don't cleanse your hands 25 times a day, but it's a nice way to help keep the bacteria away.

Why Travelling Slow Keeps You Healthier Than Travelling Fast

Again, this is all about keeping on top of your body and not getting exhausted. Proper sleep, proper nutrition and proper exercise are crucial, and frankly, when you are catching flights every other day between cities, there is no time to do anything but GO GO GO.

And GO GO GO is bad for your health. It's OK in short spurts but awful after a week.

So, another reason to travel slow is having the ability to take better care of yourself.

Remember what I said earlier about getting bored in a country? Getting a little bored ain't a bad thing because then you'll be able to focus better on your new country and you'll also be able to focus more on yourself.

If you want to make travel sustainable, slow travel is the only way. Otherwise you will burn out and feel like shit 24/7.

If you are in Moscow for two days, you are going to feel pressured to do everything you can in that two days to make the best of your trip. Fast travel forces our hands. We can either see everything in the 48 hours we have, or miss out and feel like we didn't even experience enough.

So what sounds better? Two days in Moscow to blitz through the city and see everything you can before collapsing while buying a Russian doll set?

Or take three weeks in Moscow. Get in, relax, get your bearings, find a gym, cook some healthy meals, meet locals and sprinkle in the sights over the course of your twenty one days?

If you want to travel longer (and cheaper, and overall just better), option number two is better.

In three weeks in any location, you'll get a feel for a place. Once you have this time to think, you'll have time to get healthy.

Why You Should Travel with a First Aid Kit

If you are travelling for any length of time you will probably get sick at some point. This may be because you had a dodgy curry, didn't wash your hands before eating or accidentally drank the tap water.

Most of the gear you should take in your first aid kit will be for treating illness but you should always have some first aid gear as well. If you're travelling for any length of time you will end up hiring a motorbike or scooter a few times and around half of you will end up crashing.

As mentioned in the 'motorbike safety' section, I've been in a few accidents. The helmet and shoes saved my assets, but in Vietnam I fucked up my arm pretty good.

Once I had hauled myself to my feet and worked out that I was still alive I noticed that my arm was bleeding quite a lot - the first aid kit that I always carry in my pack stopped it. When packing your first aid kit, there's a few things you need…

For injury

- Disinfectant for cuts – I prefer savlon spray
- Bandage
- Pack of Steristrips for sealing open wounds
- Gauze Tape
- An assortment of plasters

- A small pair of nail scissors – for cutting tape, nails and digging out splinters

For illness

- **Pain relief** – Ibuprofen and Paracetamol
- **Diarrhea** – Cirpofluxocillin antibiotics and rehydration sachets (if you put salt in a coke and drink it the effect is basically the same as taking a rehydration sachet)
- **Giardia (bad diarrhea)** – Metronidazole antibiotics
- **For infection** – Flucoxocillin antibiotics
- **Altitude sickness** – Diamox, aspirin
- **Vomiting and nausea** – Avomine

Don't forget personal medicine, for example I take my asthma inhaler. Obviously there are a lot of other illnesses you can get but if you have the above medicines packed away you will be able to deal with the most common problems. You can usually buy medical supplies cheaply and easily whilst travelling but it makes sense to have a well stocked first aid kit.

Getting Vaccinated

** Disclaimer - I am not a doctor.

These are my recommendations based on my personal travel experiences, but in no way is it intended to be medical advice. With this information I hope to begin to inform you so you can confidently continue to your own research and make educated decisions about which vaccinations are best for you. **

Keeping fit and healthy will keep your immune system strong, but not strong enough to fight a lethal jungle virus. At the end of the day, vaccinations can save lives.

Vaccinations are a bit of a controversial topic in the backpacking world. Lots of travellers believe them to be unnecessary, other travellers swear by them.

Personally, I'm vaccinated against everything.

Depending on which part of the world you are visiting you may need to get certain vaccinations such as Tetanus, Yellow Fever, Rabies etc. These vaccinations are expensive but last for a long time so it is best to see them as an investment. Go to your travel nurse at least three months before you are due to travel (some of the vaccinations take three months to take effect) to see what she recommends.

To me it makes sense. I live on the road and compared to slowly dying from some exotic jungle fever, it seems a small, worthy investment.

Recommended Vaccinations

- Typhoid fever is a serious disease you can get from contaminated food or water. Typhoid can cause high fever, fatigue, weakness, stomach pains, headache, loss of appetite, and sometimes a rash. If it is not treated, it can kill up to 30% of people who get it. It will set you back about $25-$50

- Tetanus is a bacterial illness commonly found in soil that manifests as headaches, painful muscle stiffness, trouble swallowing, fever, and high blood pressure. Even with intensive care, 10%–20% of people with tetanus die. Highly recommended for people doing humanitarian work in developing nations. Vaccinations cost between $20-$30.

• Rabies is a neurotropic virus that is lethal. If you are bitten by a rabid animal, you'll need to be rushed to a quality hospital for treatment within 72 hours. While the chances of being bit by an animal that's actually carrying the rabies virus are pretty low, if you travel a lot – it's worth being vaccinated. Rabies vaccines are more expensive and can cost you up to $400.

• All over the internet debate rages as to whether or not you should take anti-malarials for various parts of the world. I myself have travelled through plenty of malarial zones without taking the recommended medication and have been fine. That said I have always made sure to limit mosquito bites by wearing long sleeves around sunset, applying mosquito repellent and sleeping beneath my mosquito net whenever possible. I don't take Malaria pills, and only would if I were travelling to certain countries. Please check www.cdc.gov/malaria/travellers/country_table/a.htmlfor a world Malaria index.

Chapter Summary

Staying healthy on the road doesn't need to be daunting - but knowledge is power and in this case, power is not dying.

Most of staying healthy is common knowledge. By applying everything you've learned in this chapter, you'll significantly reduced the chances of anything unfortunate happening to you.

• Boost your immune system by working out and keeping fit! A healthy traveler is a happy traveler. You don't want to feel like shit and the best way to avoid that is taking precautions and keeping your immune system strong with good nutrition and exercise.

- Beware of the water. Drinking and brushing your teeth with dodgy water is playing with fire. Sometimes you might be OK, but eventually you will get sick.

- Clean hands are the best way to combat bacteria. Carry hand sanitizer on your travels.

- Travelling slow is travelling healthier. Travelling fast builds anxiety and creates little time for a good night's rest. By travelling slowly you'll be able to live like a normal human being and you'll have the time you need to take care of their body.

- Depending where in the world you wish to travel, I highly recommend getting proper vaccinations. Do your personal research and decide what / if you need vaccinations. Do not completely ignore vaccinations.

- Bring a small first aid kit. You won't need it often, but when you do you'll be thankful you have it

- Eat street food and similar food vendors that are popular with locals. If a vendor resembles something like a ghost town…. Maybe head to the next one! Following the locals will deliver you to the cheapest and safest food options.

- Avoid insect bites by wearing long sleeves and trousers at dawn and dusk. Sleep under a mosquito net where possible.

Chapter Nine
Making the Connection

Believe it or not, I used to be very shy.

Before my travels, I was socially awkward - in particular I found it painfully difficult to even talk to girls. I was unsure of myself, unhappy with how I looked and unconvinced on what I could offer to a conversation.

I had a fairly hard run at school and was bullied (like a lot of kids) pretty much mercilessly on account of being short and being shit at football. This had a big effect on my social development and I felt uncomfortable around most people. I was only really happy when I was windsurfing, the only sport I was good at as a kid.

The thing about travelling is that it constantly forces you out of your comfort zone. Especially if you're travelling solo in a place like India. You have to dodge cows, beggars, horrific toilets and endless train journeys on an almost daily basis.

My first travels took me around India for eighteen months, by myself without a phone or a buddy. **I came out the other side a totally different person.**

My travels to India completely reconstructed how I viewed challenges. It didn't happen overnight but it also didn't take especially long - fairly quickly I was not only happy to be by myself but I was also happy to approach a group of strangers, strike up a conversation and have a good time with people I didn't know - something which, for me, had been unthinkable before I travelled to India.

The good news is that you very quickly grow accustomed to dealing with these situations and you will grow as a person pretty damn fast. You will become more and more confident in your ability to look after yourself, to conquer your fears and to just get on with whatever the hell life throws at you.

With the ladies, my game dramatically improved (it's hard to still be scared of chatting to hot girls when you've literally conquered mountains).

The point that I'm trying to make is that travel literally changed my life. I became a totally different person and this was all because I was hit with challenges which, through perseverance, I managed to overcome.

Sure, there were odd occasions when I felt like doing a U-turn and pissing off back to England but I knew, deep down, that it would be a mistake and so I stuck it out. The good times far outweighed the bad and the bad times helped me feel significantly more confident in my ability to handle myself.

No matter how confident you are, travelling will improve your confidence and social skills and give you an opportunity to get some damn fine conversation pieces under your belt... *"Did I ever tell you about that one time in Venezuela..."*

Who to Travel With

Don't travel with ex-lovers, mortal enemies, active members of the KKK, Voldemort, or anyone that gets on your nerves.

That's the no-go list.

Aside from that, you can travel with anyone, but I

recommend giving it some serious thought!

Being family, lovers, or great friends with someone might be working for you in your current situation, but it doesn't mean it will work out as a travelling companion. Ohhh no.

This is because travelling with someone is kind of like being married to someone - except hygiene can be difficult to solve and they might smell a bit and then you'll never ever be able to get the hell away from them.

Travelling with Friends on the Road

A.K.A travelling with people you've met on your travels.

This is a natural part of your trip and trust me it will happen. It's natural, and frankly it's kind of exciting. You have you plans. They have theirs. Then all of a sudden due to luck, fate, and a few nights of drinking, you've met a new travel buddy and formed a strong friendship.

So it's easy. Travel with who you want to travel with, and bail when you want to bail.

There are no strings attached to travelling with friends you meet on the road. It's an unspoken backpacker rule - if you ever want to branch off and go solo, you are unlikely to be given a hard time.

Travelling with Friends from Home

Travelling with your best mates will be one of the most amazing bonding experiences you can have.

Your lifetime of already stellar memories is only going to increase with every city, country, and sticky situation you guys get into.

If you are thinking about travelling with your besties - go for it!

Two points I want to make though.

The first is don't depend on your besties.

Too often I have seen first time travellers make plans to travel with their besties. Not even *plans* to travel, I'm talking *blood oaths* to travel.

And often, one of the friends is very serious, and the other thinks they are serious but really aren't serious. This will usually come to light once the time has come to man up and buy tickets. The conversation will usually be like:

> Friend #1 - "Dude, are you ready! Today's the day we get our tickets to Addis Abbaba! I've been keeping an eye on the prices and the flights are so cheap! I'm so excited, we've been talking about this for months, let's do this!"
>
> Friend # 2 - "Oooooh yeah, about that. You see I know we established today as the deadline after the last deadline I missed... but remember how I told you about how uncomfortable my couch was? Well I was at IKEA and I couldn't resist, you should see it though mate, it matches the feng shui perfectly, I can't wait to get a matching coffee table once I...."

At this point friend # 1 can do one of two things.

1. Say OK! We'll put this on hold another month and get the tickets then! Denial is powerful.

2. Realize that travelling as a *we,* is never going to fucking happen.

And hear me out, friend #2 isn't a bad dude! He just has different priorities. He might want to travel, he just isn't quite as ready as friend #1.

So, if you are friend #1, I beg of thee, do not wait for friend #2. They will never turn around, and frankly, you don't need them at all to travel.

Stick to your deadlines. If you guys agree to purchase your tix on a certain day - you purchase that shit no matter what!

The second point I want to make about travelling with besties.

Travelling with someone is a commitment. I said earlier it's like marrying someone. There'll be lots of fun, but when you are travelling with someone, you are with them 24/7. You travel on buses together, you sleep in hostels together, you book airline tickets together, you see sights together, you meet new people together. It's endless!

And what can happen, is that any small thing that annoys you about them (and them about you) will amplify.

It won't happen after a week. But if you travel with someone long term (think three months plus) you are going to discover exactly the type of person that they really are, and anything that irks you about them could begin to plague you.

You could hypothetically separate from one another, but newbie travel partnerships rarely do.

Which is why I recommend - DO IT!

Spend some time away from each other! Go on a walk by yourself. Go see a sight by yourself! Take a couple of days off from each other…

Travel is just as much about your personal experience as much as it is the dual-experience.

And please - make a backup plan. Just. In. Case.

This sort of backup plan should be made by everyone travelling with others, and only utilized in the most dire of circumstances. But create an exit plan. So if your travel partner is annoying the living hell out of you, you can get out of there and continue to travel without feeling the need to murder them.

Specifically, before the trip starts, plant a seed. Try something like this...

"I cannot wait for this trip! AH! It's going to be so cool! But you know, I gotta be honest... there's something I've been feeling inside that's been poking at me... This strange desire to travel alone... to really challenge myself and see what it's like... It's just a strange feeling. Have you ever felt that?"

Then, change the conversation to a completely different subject.

What have you just done?

You've given yourself an exit plan.

You've brought up the desire to travel solo in a very very subtle way. You aren't saying that you are going to do it. But the thought has been *'poking at'* you.

This gives you an easy way out. Let's say after two and a half months your travel partners constant _____*(insert insufferable personal attribute here)*_____ pushes you too far. You can then calmly bring up that one time, and how the feeling has been intensifying.

Note; the subtle solo travel hint is only recommended for friends, not relationships. I can't imagine many girlfriends being thrilled with such a personal revelation. Relationship travel has its own set of recommendations...

Travelling in a Relationship

There's a saying... travelling long term in a relationship will **make** or **break** you. Backpacking the world as a couple **will be** the most most challenging / rewarding thing you ever do. And it's likely that at the end of your trip one of two things will happen.

You'll either get married and be together forever... or break up (that is if you haven't strangled each other already).

Many couples have tried to travel together. Many have succeeded, many have failed. As with travelling with friends, travelling with a significant other will amplify anything about them you might find annoying.

It's actually a great test to see overall compatibility! In my opinion, everyone who's thinking about getting married should travel the world with their SO for at least three months. If you make it through that, put a ring on it! It's a match made in heaven!

Similar to travelling with besties, if you are going to travel with a SO, make sure to consciously create alone time. It will save your relationship and just as important, your sanity.

If while in Sri Lanka, you meet a group of girls travelling from India and your lady love gets on with them, let them have a girl's night out!

If while in Toronto your hunk-o-man gets on well with some outstanding chaps from Bermuda, let them have a boy's night out!

The other half can stay back, recharge the batteries, smash out a book, and get some much needed rest / alone time...

A lot of newbie backpackers are a tad scared to travel alone and end up dragging a mate or SO other along for the ride even though they strongly suspect it isn't going to work out... If you have that feeling then do NOT drag somebody along, instead; take a deep breath, realise that this is the right call and head out solo. You won't regret it.

Embracing Backpacker Culture

Backpacker culture has its fair share of flaws. Believe me, there are some things that backpackers do that make my blood boil - Never get on an elephant!

But more over less, backpacker culture / lifestyle is a smashing good time!

And it gets better once you embrace it. Don't fight it. Don't roll your eyes when the billionth persons asks you where you've been and where you're going next. It's all a part of the process baby!

In general, us backpackers are a friendly bunch and with this next ultimate travel hack, I'm going to teach you how to make friends with other travellers no matter where you are...

The 'Universal Amigo Maker' (with tips)

So maybe you are especially socially awkward. Let's run through some conversational tips that will have you transformed into a backpacking social butterfly in no time.

First off - I'd say a decent majority backpackers are creative-like introverts.

You'll get the dominant males, you'll get the flashpacker divas, and every now and then you'll come across a very loud group of twats that over the course of a few cities have magnetized together like some sort of nightmarish transformer that won't shut the hell up.

But mostly, travellers are very down to earth and chilled people. So, if you are too, fear them not! You are amongst your people.

There's a very intricate system of communication that happens with backpackers. There's a flow. Let me teach you.

If you're feeling social and wish to engage in conversation, there is a go-to that ALWAYS works.

Simply...

"Hi! Where are you from?"

You don't need to introduce yourself, you don't need some epic social strategy, this is all you need.

"Hey! Where are you from?"

Once you ask that, you can sit back and let the magic happen.

Now from there, I can basically guarantee where the conversation will go next. If you were in a hotel or plane you might ask *"business or pleasure?"* or if you were at a social or networking event you might say something like *"oh, how do you know the organizer?"*

But when you are in a hostel, these questions don't work. They are here for the same reasons you are - to travel. And they know the same people you know - no one.

So from here, the conversation will naturally progress to...

"Where did you come from?"

Now, there are variations to this question, but it always means the same thing... which country / city were you travelling in before this?

This is always fun because chances are your circuits are similar, or maybe even better, you are heading to the country they just got back from!

BOOM!

Instant connection.

And if that doesn't work, the inevitable next backpacker question…

"Where are you headed to next?"

And of course, the ultimate question…

"How long are you travelling for?"

The great thing about these questions is they give people a chance to talk about themselves on a topic which EVERYBODY in the room can relate to, anybody can join in and that's the beauty of it. I've had this same conversation over a thousand times, but it never really gets old. It's a great way of making new amigos.

Getting along with other independent travellers is pretty easy. Unlike home where you'll be surrounded by people who might be difficult to connect with, independent travellers all have a shared interest in one thing.

A love for Jesus.

Just kidding. Travel. Not Jesus.

Hence the conversation pointers from before. You can immediately bond with other backpackers knowing that you'll share a mutual interest in backpacking the world. This bond will enable you to immediately converse and connect with everyone who crosses your path.

Dorm Etiquette

There are some serious dos and don'ts in hostels. This part is basically highlighting all of the things NOT to do.

These are the basic standards of dorm-politeness

Lights and Noise

Nights at hostels can be a mess. Usually half of the guests are winding down around 10pm (the non-partiers) and the other half of the guests are just perking up (the partiers).

In a perfect world, the noise and party would be taken out of the dorm rooms, but this isn't always the case.

So what I recommend for you is to lead by example. After 10pm, be quiet and courteous in hostel dorms.

This includes a huge pet peeve - don't turn on the lights!

Often the light switch of a hostel dorm will turn a dark, quiet area into more of a well-lit stadium. Use your phone, head torch, sense of touch… try not to flood a dark dorm room with blinding light.

Don't Touch Anyone's Stuff

Someone leaves their backpack on your bunk? Sure, gently place it on the floor. But otherwise there is no reason to ever touch someone else's gear.

This is especially true with the bathroom and kitchen.

Don't use someone else's toothpaste, don't go in the community fridge and eat anyone else's food.

Only touch what is yours.

Dealing with Snoring

There's no way around it. If you are paying the cheapest lodging price available for a hostel dorm bed, you are paying for everything that comes with that.

And one of the things in fine print you may have missed is the fact that people snore in hostels.

So instead of fighting it! Let's look at ways to improve the situation.

1. You can pay for a solo room, or always camp or Couchsurf (where you'll likely have a couch to sleep on, away from any snorers).

2. Pop in some headphones or earbuds.

Headphones aren't always comfortable to sleep with, but after a few nights you'll get used to them. Listen to some music, or download some soothing sounds of ocean waves or soft rain or some other hippy stuff... it'll be much preferable to the chainsaw-snoring right next to you.

Also, if someone is snoring, it's OK to nudge them.

I know that sounds a bit aggressive, but it isn't.

If someone has a bad snoring problem, they probably know it, and they probably know it because they've been told and nudged in their sleep a hundred times by ex-lovers or family members.

Once someone is snoring, it means they are in a deep sleep. A little *'hey bud you're snoring pretty loud'* with a light nudge can hopefully get them to shift to their stomach or side.

Sleeping on stomach or side = no snoring.

Sexy Time

Mmmmm it's about to get real juicy up in here.

Actually, sex in dorms is far from that. It's usually sloppy, annoying, and pumped with hard liquor.

If you must get it on while staying in a dorm, do NOT

have sex in the dorm room.

It is classless, it is loud, it is just down right rude.

If there is nowhere to go, the first place is the bathroom. Next check the showers.

See if there's a private area outside. Scope it out. But please, no matter what, do not bang in the bunk bed. It will wake everyone up and make the situation extremely uncomfortable.

If you hook up with someone once, and foresee a second, third, fourth, etc time - do yourself both a favor and get a private room! Splitting the cost will make it cheap and then you can do it like they do on the discovery channel all night without keeping anyone else awake.

Pre-Packing the Night Before

This should be carved in stone at the head of every hostel.

Often flights leave early, which means you'll have to get to the airport early, which means you'll have to wake up early.

So what sounds better? Waking up at 5am to pack all of your gear for 30 minutes? Or waking up at 5:30 am with everything ready to go?

I'll tell you, in the opinion of everyone else in the dorm, option #2 sounds better, because it literally sounds better (not noisy).

Mornings are very quiet in hostels. Don't be that obnoxious backpacker ruining everyone else's peace by reorganizing all of your belongings, opening plastic bags, unzipping zippers, popping containers open and closed and so on and so on.

Do yourself and everyone else in the dorm a huge favour -

pack up the night before.

Befriend Thy Neighbors

Introducing yourself to every bed mate in the seventeen person dorm is not necessary, but introducing yourself to the person above, below, to the right, or left of you is **highly** recommended.

It's good manners to introduce yourself, but it's also smart to make friends with those who are sleeping next to you and literally closest to you.

You can help keep an eye on their stuff and they'll do the same for you. If anything suspicious happens, you got each other's backs.

But regardless, please know that every one of these rules **will** be broken...

No matter what, all of these rules will be broken *extensively* on your travels. The only way to combat the noise and chaos and take control of what's happening in your brain is to bring headphones. Stock it with music, podcasts, audio books - whatever!

Because when Joe and Molly got a bit too drunk and decide to have a root in the extra-echoey bathroom, and Cecil, your Spanish bed mate is snoring like a chainsaw, and Edra and Bethany the Israelis are taking shots and smoking a joint right outside the door, and Constantine tops it all off by packing his entire life for two hours to catch his 4am flight back to Moscow....

You can take some control, pop in your headphones, and at least hear noises that you enjoy.

When It's OK to Tell People to Piss Off

It's very rare to be in this situation. Because of the fast-friend nature of backpacking, you can slide in and out of any social situation you are in with great ease.

But every now and again, you'll find yourself in a situation, with someone, and you just need them to back off.

I remember once in Prague, I had spent a week hitchhiking across Germany and camping out. I rocked up to the city to crash for a night in a hostel. I went to sleep around 1am, as did most of the dorm.

We were all awoken at 3:30 in the morning when two horrifically loud and drunk Aussie lads slammed into the room, turned on the lights and started messing around. I remained calm for about a minute. Then, one of them sat on my bed, and began eating a hotdog. That's not a euphemism.

I instantly began shouting at him to get the fuck out of the dorm and was backed up by everybody else present. It was a victory but I was fuming... this is the problem with dorms, every now and again you have to deal with people like this.

If you're a long term traveler, it's not just other backpackers who you will sometimes have to yell at. In India for example, touts are a real problem and some of the more persistent ones will attempt to grab you in a death-grip handshake.

They know that it's instinctive to shake an offered hand and once they have yours... they don't let go. They instead try to sell you some shit. Sometimes with these guys, you need to tell them to back the fuck off. The same goes for taxi drivers trying to rip you off.

Don't get me wrong, 99% of the people you meet on your

travels will be awesome. You just need to remember that there are some less nice people out there. In general, shouting at them will get rid of them. Only break this little party trick out of the bag when it's absolutely necessary as, in general, you can get away with a stern *'I will not be screwed with'* voice.

Respecting Local Culture

I respect your opinions and views, and similarly I hope you would respect mine! I'm certain you believe certain things, and reject others.

But when you are in a foreign country, your opinion means less.

When you are visiting a new region of the world, what you believe matters, but the local customs come first and completely trump your personal vindications.

When you travel, the culture of the country you are in is more important than your own beliefs. It's a matter of respect and personal safety. If you can't handle it and can't keep your mouth shut, don't visit countries with cultural aspects you condone.

If you find traditional Islam's mandate of hijabs to be oppressive to women, this is not an opinion you can voice out loud - not unless it is bought up by a local person.

If you are in a Muslim country, you better a) wear a hijab (don't do this if you're a man) and b) be quiet about your differing beliefs.

When you go to a new country, it's an unspoken rule that you will maintain a respectful attitude about the customs even if you don't totally agree or understand how things are done in this part of the world.

Why You Should Be Making Backpacker Friends

When you travel, you'll meet interesting people from all over the world, and often find out that they are heading in the same direction as you – boom, instant travel buddy. Another very cool perk to this is that as you make friends from all over the world, you will have a lot of people to visit on your future travels.

This is another one of those 'best of backpacking' things you don't really hear about. As you make lifelong friends from the Philippines, Croatia, Ecuador and wherever else, you now have couches to sleep on in the Philippines, Croatia, Ecuador and wherever else. I've crashed on more couches than I could count from friends I've made on the road. It's really cool to see them after months or years, trade stories, and build upon an already strong foundation.

Why You Should Be Making Local Friends

While backpackers are likely some of the most open minded people in the world, some travelers only seem interested in befriending other travelers – which is a massive shame.

Maybe it's fear or language barriers or whatever, but truth be told, some of the best people I've met on my travels have been locals.

I've couchsurfed over a hundred times, staying in local homes and getting to know local people. Some of my best friends are Pakistani and Iranian. I have good amigos in Japan, Turkey, Thailand and Georgia...

Locals are awesome friends because they know where to find the hidden gems. They know the best spots to eat, the best spots to drink, they know the places the tourists go that suck, and most importantly, they know the places that tourists *don't go* that are awesome.

Making friends with local people, and seeing a country through their unique viewpoint, is one of the highlights of travel. You will often experience and see things that would be impossible without local help - like the time I crashed out in a cave in Jordan with a Rastafarian Bedouin. He showed me something that is not published in any guidebook - a totally hidden canyon leading to ancient ruins outside of Petra's national Park.

Another great place to make local friends is at your hostel. Locals will own, run and manage your hostel and they will usually be trustworthy, familiar with backpacker culture and very easy to connect with – usually anyway!

Have a chat with the cute local chick at the front desk, seriously – do it. Ask the bartender for some food recommendations. Making friends with locals and having experiences with locals is crucial. It turns a backpacking experience into a human and cultural experience. Partying with other backpackers all the time – that isn't a rounded travel experience.

You won't know the real meaning of travel until a local invites you to their house for dinner. Once you have experienced that, you have earned a new travel badge.

Smashing Language Barriers

If you are reading this, it means you have some fluency in English, so you've already got a jump start. English is the international language, and will be a great stepping stone for communication. Most people around the world speak a bit of English but if you truly want to connect, you need to make a proper effort to learn the local lingo.

If you are travelling slowly, it's a great idea to learn some of the language. Don't overwhelm yourself by trying to achieve fluency, but making an effort to speak the language of the locals will greatly benefit you.

The locals will be very pleased that you respected their culture and language enough to make an effort, and obviously that can help you in general – at the very least it usually makes it easier to get a better deal when haggling.

If you don't speak the local language, attempting to communicate with people might seem intimidating - but don't let it be! The best way to smash language barriers is with the universal language.

Hand signals and a genuine smile!

You'd be surprised how well we can communicate with our hands. Body language + something relevant to point at + sincerity = language barriers no more!

We are all human beings, make the effort to connect.

Love on the Road

So as you'll be making friends (both local and other travellers), you'll eventually run into a few that you want to have sex with.

You are going to meet people that you are attracted to, people who will hopefully also be attracted to you. And given the nature of independent travel (free spirited, living in the moment) romances happen, and they happen often.

Do your thing - I'm not trying to get into your love life, I just want to make a quick point.

Travel relationships can be very, very powerful. And that power can be both a great thing, and something to be cautious about.

It's a good thing because this is what life's all about! Love and passion are experiences many people have on the road, and I've met numerous couples who met while travelling to areas of the world that were foreign to both of them.

What I do want to say though - is tread lightly. Try to keep a rational frame of mind.

Due to the passion and power of travel relationships, people often drastically change, or abandon their travel plans all together! While sometimes it is true love, sometimes the power of the moment can be blinding, especially when trying to evaluate someone you haven't really known very long at all.

And because of this, things can move quickly. Ten days ago you were travelling the world solo... Now you're basically living with someone who may or may not be a bit mental and, before you know it, you're both alcoholics.

I'm not discouraging love on the road. I've had my share of travel flings - they're great!

Just don't lose yourself in the power of feelings when

travelling with someone else. Due to the lonely nature of travelling solo, the intoxication of love can be particularly potent when backpacking.

Chapter Summary

While the sights are going to blow your mind, I'd have to say that the most memorable experiences you have whilst travelling will be of the people you meet on the road. Making a connection with other travellers is usually pretty easy. You'll meet new friends, lovers and everything in between.

- Backpacking the world will introduce you to lifelong friends. If you travel right, these friends will be a healthy mix of other travellers and locals. The experiences with these folks will be the highlights of your travels.

- Because of this, you never really travel alone. Often we think travelling solo will be harrowingly lonely, but it's just not the case. Between fast hostel friends and lifelong travel companions, you're only a 'Hey, where are you from?' from a great social interaction.

- Travelling solo is my highest recommendation, but if you decide to travel with someone, be 100% sure it's the right person. This applies to family, friends, lovers, husbands, wives, mistresses, and everything in between.

- Love and sex happens on the road. Romances can feel very powerful. Have a good time, just keep everything in perspective.

Chapter Ten
Solo Travel
(and Why You Should Give it a Go)

You can do whatever you want

An enormous part of the desire to travel is the desire to achieve complete and unabashed freedom. I mean if freedom is what you are looking, holy shit you should get excited.

Imagine days on the beach, in some foreign village, or trekking deep into shining mountains or through a steaming jungle. You are alive, you are smiling, you are in the moment… and in this moment, you smile realizing…

You have nothing you *have* to do.

You have nowhere you *have* to be.

You have no one to report to.

You have no one to compromise with.

You are free to do anything and everything that pleases you.

You want to do _____ today? Do it.

You want to do _____ tomorrow? Do it.

Are you noticing a pattern here?

Travelling with buddies is great, but there's something relentlessly rewarding about travelling solo. It's certainly not without it's struggles (more on that in a bit) but it's one of the greatest gifts you can give to yourself.

You have no baggage, no reputation, no expectations, no

nothing.

Just a backpack and the freedom to do anything you like.

Well not anything - solo travel isn't a free pass to leverage anonymity to be a twat. This isn't Westworld, this is the real world, but you get what I mean.

Solo ≠ Alone

And as mentioned earlier, if you're feeling a bit more social, you will have every opportunity to meet people and gain new friends.

When you travel solo you'll sometimes get what's dubbed in the sales world as "The Jones effect".

The Jones Effect means when people see someone doing something, they want to do it as well!

So remember your friend from chapter nine? The one you made the blood oath with to travel the world forever but got distracted by IKEA furniture?

Well guess what.

Your bestie has been stalking your Instagram pics for the past month and now wants to meet you on the road! He's only got enough money for a month, but figures he'll meet you at your next stop and travel a few weeks with you!

Woohoo!

Friends who want to travel will see you as an inspiration and opportunity to overcome their own fears. They aren't using you. You have just enabled them to get a grip and to take their own plunge and, chances are, they admire you big time for hitting the road before them.

This is far from a guarantee, but I've seen it happen often

and have had numerous amigos come and join me for some real adventuring on their holidays.

How to Enjoy Alone Time

One incorrect notion aspiring travellers have, is that of time.

Aspiring travellers envision themselves travelling in a nonstop GO GO GO - seeing sights, catching planes, and going bar hopping every night of the week.

While it's true that you will do many of these things, the truth is, if you are travelling slowly (as I recommend you do) you are going to have a ton of spare time on your hands.

You're going to have more time than you can possibly even think you are going to have. Sure, when you get to Marrakech you'll go see the sights you've been dying to see and maybe go on that desert trek you've been saving up for...

But what about all the time in between?

I'm telling you, you'll have twice as much down time than you will active time. Not to mention all the long times waiting. Waiting for buses to arrive. Waiting for buses to depart. Waiting for a lift on the side of the road. Waiting for the 5 o'clock tour to start. Waiting in airports. Waiting on that guy to bring you weed. Waiting for the sun to set. Waiting for the sun to rise. There will be a lot of waiting!

This is the part of the chapter where other people might recommend chilling out in your dorm room and watching some Netflix. For much of the world, time to kill equals Netflix and chill.

I wholeheartedly reject this.

Sure, the random Game of Thrones binge aside, I try and

limit my movie / TV consumption while travelling. The whole point of travelling is to engage and interact and have new experiences in new parts of the world! Not to slip into the same routine of killing time that you were stuck in back home.

Just because you are travelling that doesn't mean you are experiencing travel. I've seen many travellers who are so glued to their phones throughout their entire trip that I genuinely wonder if they are really seeing anything that is unfurling around them.

For the love of Jebus, Don't waste your time on Facebook, Instagram or Snapchat.... Sure, throw out a social media update here and there, but you can do that anywhere in the world and being glued to your phone is a sure-fire way to miss out on the experience of being abroad. Limit your phone-time.

I want to encourage you to get off and stay off your phones. When I hit the road for the first time, I didn't have a phone – and it was glorious.

So what are you going to do with all this new free/alone time?

There is no better opportunity to learn and practice a new skill.

Read

The easiest thing to do in all of your spare time is to read. If you've bought a kindle, you'll put it to good use.

I crush books when on the road. It's amazing. You just chill and pass the days balls deep in your favorite novels.

A cool backpacker tradition is the good ole' book exchange. Travel with a book. Read it. Once you've finished it you can exchange it at a hostel (they always have leftover books) or trade with another traveler (very common). This is a great way to keep your bag light (books are heavy) and keep entertained. Here's a list of books worth checking out:

www.thebrokebackpacker.com/best-books-to-read-while-travelling/

Get fit

If you've got an extra couple hours a day and you don't know what to do - get shredded!

You can find places to exercise and make fitness a big goal. We talked about how to stay fit earlier, but if you want to make this a goal, you'll have plenty of time to get jacked.

Journal

While you could document your travels on a blog, there's something so much more intimate about a journal. Not to mention that publishing your craziest travel-tales might give Grandma a heart attack - some stories are best kept secret.

Yes, keeping a journal while travelling is a bit of a cliché, but you'll thank me when you have that sturdy moleskin to help document your experiences and pass the time.

Any Skill! (I'm really serious here!)

Practice yoga. Learn how to dive. Start drawing. Learn how to spin fire poi. Write the book you've always dreamt of. Do standup comedy around the world. Make a documentary. Discover new music around the world. Write handwritten letters to friends and family. Study a subject that interests you.

Achieve fluency in a new language.

There are literally endless amounts of things you can do with your new alone time. Just hone in on something that interests you, and go balls to the wall! Look at this time as a golden opportunity to pursue something of value, a time to achieve a new skill or perfect a new personal craft - how often do we get the chance to do that?

Starting a Web Presence

If the idea of being a Digital Nomad interests you - now is the time to spring into action.

My first seven years of travelling I did a lot of different things, but I didn't start my travel blog until a few years ago.

Once I put my mind to it, it became clear to me that now that I was travelling full time, I had the time and resources to give the whole blogging game a real stab. Time is key here – without the time and energy to invest, you will not get anywhere online.

The greatest way to build a Digital Nomad lifestyle is through a life of travel – it's actually easier to build an online income whilst on the road as opposed to from your home country, 95% of the time anyway.

You get to live for significantly cheaper than you would at home, and when you **do** need to find work, options exist that can fit your needs.

What sounds better? Working 40+ hours a week at home to pay your bills, break even, and maybe find some time to build your online business?

Or.

Travel the world, live on the cheap, get an almost

unlimited amount of time to work on your projects, and pick up work when needed.

Downsides of Solo Travel

Whilst the benefits of solo travel are many, there can be some disadvantages....

The first downside people speak of when travelling alone is fear of missing out and loneliness. But as we talked about already, that loneliness is more of a perceived loneliness. You'll have every opportunity to meet new and interesting people from around the world.

Also, when travelling with a friend, the security is nice. Having someone to watch your back (and you theirs) is great! It helps take the edge off, particularly for tech worries and theft.

This is especially true when in transit. Whether at an airport, bus stop, or hitching through a new town - when you have someone you trust, you don't have to carry your gear around everywhere.

Bathroom run? Leave your stuff - friends got it in their sights! Quick bite to eat? Leave your stuff - friends got it covered!

Because when you are alone, you have to drag all of your gear everywhere, and well frankly, that can get downright irritating – especially if you need to use the bathroom on an Indian sleeper train.

And surprisingly, solo travel can sometimes cost you more!

While hostels are popular in many regions of the world, they flat out don't exist in other parts of the world.

Countries like Pakistan, Iran and Venezuela don't really have much of a hostel scene, and if you don't camp and can't find a Couchsurfing host - you'll have to pay for accommodation the good old fashioned way. An inn or a guesthouse. And they usually ain't cheap.

Splitting costs with another traveler can be beneficial. You can split rooms, but there are other things you can go halves on.

Taxis become so much more affordable when there's two people. Cutting the rate in half makes taxis seem less terrifying to the budget.

Bulk cooking is easier with two people, which can cut down food costs if you are staying in one place for a while.

So while travelling solo has many incredible benefits, it might cost you a bit more in certain situations.

First Week Travelling - Survival Tips

The greatest challenge as a first time solo traveler is overcoming the anxiety you may experience during your first week on the road.

Your nerves will be all over the place, you'll be alone, you'll be bloody excited and bloody scared, all while in a foreign country far from home.

First things first buddy.

Breeaattthhhheeee.

Long breathe in. Hold it. Long breathe out. Repeat.

The first week may be a mental and emotional clusterfuck of an experience. Just accept that it's going to be a bit of a wild ride...

But after a few days you will get your bearings, and everything will be fine.

Human beings are incredible in our ability to adapt - it just takes a bit to get settled into something new.

The best piece of advice I can give you, especially if you are a bit of a shy introvert, is to start talking to people!

This is the best way to get things going. You'll meet cool people, and they'll distract you from whatever you're anxious about. Many people you'll meet on the road may have travelled before, so they might even take you under their wing a bit. If not, chances are they are newbies to and you are in the same situation.

The best way to get chatting this is to set an actionable goal. When I was in India, my goal was to talk to five new people every day for a minimum of one minute. Doing so got me talking to many new people and rapidly increased my confidence.

You're going to love it, so much that after the first couple of weeks you'll probably never want to go back to your 9/5. You'll love travel, so much... that you might want to do it more (cough; forever)...

Chapter Summary

- Backpacking the world might not be as fast paced as you anticipate. There will be lots of downtime and you should look at that downtime as a once in a lifetime opportunity to master something.
- Try to identify your likes to help figure out what it is you want to get better at. Whatever you choose, go at

it with one hundred and ten percent.

- Get your read on. If you like to read, you'll fall in love with this style of travel. If you aren't much of a reader - give it a go! All of the times you have to wait for something (buses, airplanes, weed deliveries) can now be looked at as another few chapters of your new book.

- Solo travel can sometimes be more expensive. Take advantage of the times you have a travel buddy, and when solo, try and remember that you might have to dish out a little bit more on accommodation and transport in certain situations.

- The first week will seem like a big blur of insanity. Be prepared for the transition, and just breathe. Go slowly and accept that whatever happens will happen, and everything will get much, much easier in a very short time.

Chapter Eleven
So You Want to Travel Forever?

Travel will probably change your life (it changed mine).

Actually, on second thought, I don't think that travel will *probably* change your life.

I think it will *definitely* change your life.

As long as you give it a chance… Go for a decent duration, challenge yourself appropriately, get off your damn phone, live in the moment.

Long term travel will definitely have an effect on you. You will see and experience new things and grow and develop as a person, which ultimately will lead to a change in your life.

The question is, how drastic a change will it be?

For me, it was probably as drastic as possible. I came out of India as a completely different person. And I wanted more.

More challenges, more personal development, more beautiful sites, all of it. So I kept travelling.

This isn't unique to me.

Often people will go on their first trip, travel for a few months, and eventually go back into the *real world* to find a *real job* (whatever the hell that means).

The thing that happens though, is that 95% of the time, those same people end up feeling their feet itch again.

This brings us back to the *Wanderlust* topic from before.

Cue cliché travel blogger talking about wanderlust being this incurable disease.

Only, the problem is... sometimes cliché travel bloggers are right.

Call it wanderlust, call it a love for travel, call it a need to experience, any name you put on it, it doesn't matter!

95% of people that get a taste of travel, become full-fledged travel addicts.

It doesn't mean they become Digital Nomads. It doesn't mean they end up travelling the world till they croak. It doesn't mean they figure it out.

But you better believe they want to.

And if I may be so bold, that's probably an enormous reason why you are here to begin with.

Once you get a taste for travel (or if you haven't yet but feel it SCREAMING your name) you will never be the same. I hate to build on clichés, but this one has the scientific data to back it up.

So while it's not a guarantee that travel will completely alter the state of your existence, there's a good chance it will have a profound impact on the way you want to live your life. And there's a good chance it'll make you want to travel indefinitely.

It *is* Possible to Travel Indefinitely – If You Want It Enough

So you're nearly through this book and you're thinking to yourself, "OK, I'm gonna travel, and realistically I've got a 50/50 shot of returning to a normal life after."

But just in case you don't want to return to normal life, let's talk about perpetual travel.

Perpetual travel is more than possible, and the longer you are on the road the better you get at it... but there's still a financial sweet spot that you need to hit. And you have to accept that while travelling broke is the greatest adventure in the world... it's difficult to sustain forever.

I travelled on less than ten dollars a day for six years. And I can tell you that whilst it was an amazing experience, I got to a point where change was needed. I wanted a better living standard. You might as well.

So while I don't think being broke should be a barrier to travelling, I think it's just as important to learn how to make money *while* you are travelling broke.

As we discussed, there are so many ways to do this; from picking up work on a bar to crewing a yacht across the world, working in farms or picking up well paying gigs in Australia.

But the thing about all of these options is that you still have to work for somebody else.

If you want total freedom, you need to work for yourself, only that way can you reap the full benefit of your hard work. Working for myself, and working hard, is one of the greatest joys I have ever known. If you want to know that joy too, an online career is the most obvious option open to you that will enable you to earn money whilst you travel.

Digital Nomad Life 101

Ok, so you've heard me mention this Digital Nomad malarkey a few times. What the hell is a Digital Nomad?

In the most basic sense, a Digital Nomad is someone who makes money online (Digital) while travelling the world (Nomad).

On the Digital side, Digital Nomads leverage the internet and make money in a variety of ways, including, but not limited to freelancing, web designing, blogging, consulting, or a variety of online entrepreneurial ventures.

Out of all the options, travel blogging is probably the best known. This is for a few reasons. Travel blogging sounds like an enviable life (and it can be!) and popular travel bloggers typically have MASSIVE social media following (because who doesn't like an epic IG photo?).

But just because it's popular doesn't mean it's the best. Truth be told, travel blogging has always been a tough path to income, and it's becoming exponentially more difficult by the day. It's become an oversaturated market and while there's a bit of money, it's tough to make great money.

There are much more lucrative ways to make money online that require a lot less time.

On the Nomads side, Digital Nomads typically aren't millionaires. They can make great money, but often are making good money. But good money by Western standards is great money by developing nations standards. For this reason, Digital Nomads have a tendency to live and travel in countries with a low cost of living.

Now here's the deal - I don't want to overwhelm you. You're here to learn the basics of travel. You are at step one, and we need to focus on one step at a time.

But. There was no way I could leave this out.

To skip past the vast opportunities offered by the digital nomad revolution would be a complete disservice, and frankly it would be unethical of me!

When it comes to travelling, being a Digital Nomad is the Bee's Knees.

While work exchanging, bartending in hostels and teaching English are all super cool they don't hold a candle to working online, as your own boss, with the freedom to move around as you please.

How Much Can Digital Nomads Make?

It took me about a year to start earning a relatively easy passive income of about $1,000 a month from my blog. This meant that whenever I wanted a beer, I had nothing to worry about. It was great!

I knew some bloggers were making six figures but I was perfectly content. My travel costs were pretty low which meant that most months I was actually saving money whilst travelling the world.

Then after another six months, my travel blog was making between $1500 and $2500 a month which was great, but it was inconsistent and I was usually spending more than I was earning as I was investing heavily into building my online presence.

Making money from a travel blog is not easy, the market is saturated and immature and therefore extremely vulnerable to manipulation by low-balling clients.

So because of this, if you want to make good money travel blogging, you will find yourself increasingly chained to your laptop. It's a hustle that never ends.

I decided that this had to change if I am to get the best

experience out of the actual travelling – which was the point of starting the blog in the first place.

Now I'm putting my Digital Nomad career into sixth gear.

My objective is to experiment with different ways of making money online that are totally unrelated to travel blogging; I'm launching a drop-shipping venture and am setting up a few amazon niche websites. I hope to hit a combined income of $10,000 a month by December 2017.

I want people to know that living a life of travel while running successful online businesses is completely possible. I'll be blogging about the whole experience with complete transparency – whether it's a massive success or a pitiful failure.

The objective here (besides hoping to make a lot of money) is to do a series of experiments into different digital nomad professions. Then, I can provide you with a blueprint so that you too can live the lifestyle you deserve. A lifestyle of endless opportunities and endless travels.

I want to build my online business to a point where I have a passive income of 10k a month. This is the magic number.

This will let me save 5k a month which I will put towards buying some land and opening a truly unique (off the grid and away from the internet) hostel somewhere in South America in a couple of years time.

If you are interested in building an online business, keep up to date with Ditch Your Desk (see URL in back of book) where I'll be recording my online ventures so you too can learn how to ditch your desk and earn money whilst travelling.

The key to travelling indefinitely

Is by making money online. You can travel broke for a while, you can hop around the world teaching English for a while, you can WWOOF around the globe until you've shovelled twenty tons of cow crap across every continent... but you'll burn out.

This is why the sustainable way to travel is by becoming a Digital Nomad.

This lifestyle is not for everyone (see; people that hate looking at computers), but if you are interested in obtaining 100% freedom – the best option is to start an online income.

And as you get better and better, eventually it is possible to build yourself a totally automated, totally passive online income that only requires about four to six hours work a week for you to bring in 10k a month... It sounds too good to be true, but it is true – if you put in the work.

Chapter Summary

The sky's the limit with the internet and as you learn more, test more and invest more, you will continue to get better and better results from your online business. The masterstroke is automating it so you can get on with living an amazing lifestyle of travel.

- Perpetual travel might not interest you - and that's fine! Just know that if at any point you change your mind, you'll have plenty of opportunity to stay on the road as long as you so please – if you put in the work.

- If you decide you want to travel indefinitely, creating an online income is your best bet. Ditching your desk full time requires income, and being a Digital Nomad is the best way to achieve that.
- There are hundreds of different paths for you to achieve financial and geographical freedom… all you have to do is pick one, buckle down and get started.
- If you want to know more about making money from your laptop, visit Ditch Your Desk.

Chapter Twelve
Returning Home

Eventually, you will have to face the inevitable. Eventually, the time will come to put on your bedraggled backpack for the last time on the road and to begin your journey home. As you look out the window, the landscape zooming by, no doubt you will be reflecting on your adventure.

Perhaps you wish you could have travelled longer, or perhaps you are excited to return home and feel that the time is right. No matter how you feel, going home is not without its challenges…

Reverse Culture Shock…

Is a real thing!

Coming back home can be difficult. For me, it's now more difficult than setting off on a fresh adventure.

After travelling the world, home might not feel the same. It's like the volume got turned down. You simply don't receive the same sensory stimulation, and even if you love your hometown, you might be surprised to now find it bland and predictable.

Don't get me wrong! Seeing friends and family and the

dogs - all good stuff!

Even just sleeping in your own bed, watching TV, drinking a cider or walking your dogs can be a nice change of pace as, let's face it, travelling can be tiring.

But for me, I've found the feeling to be short-lived. The first two days I'm like *'yeaaa home!'*. After two weeks I'm like *'get me the heck outta here!'*

Most people I know feel similarly. It's because you'll want to experience life as you did on the road - raw and evolving.

Often, once home, people find it difficult to connect with friends as you have such different things to talk about - you want to talk about your travels but are now in danger of one-upping all of their stories.

Nobody wants every hangout to be dominated by Captain Adventure.

And at times, you might find it difficult to get people to relate to your new perspectives.

Also, re-adjusting to western prices sucks and it takes time to stop obsessing over prices - when I went home after India, I was still working in rupees... when I realised a beer cost 400 rupees, the same as a bottle and a half of quality Indian rum, I struggled to come to terms with wasting my money.

Learning from Your Travels

Your travels are going to teach you so much about yourself. It will strengthen you, and given you a new arsenal of skills - adaptability, patience, and a heightened ability to solve problems and create solutions.

When you get back home, I suggest you do some soul

searching. Really meditate on what's important to you. If travel is the answer, then you can begin taking the necessary steps to make it happen again.

Now that you have these new skills, don't let them go to waste, use them!

If you're ready to settle down back home - that's great! The goal is happiness, and whether your happiness is most amplified in Havana, Hanoi or Home, as long as you are happy, you've won!

So if home is victory for you, use your newly developed skills. Now is the time to land your dream job. You'll have the self-awareness and confidence to make it work. Do it!

And if home isn't for you, and you want to travel more - then use your skills!

You are a go-getter now. You are a problem solver. Don't mislead yourself into believing you *have to* live a life you don't want to live.

If you are home and want to travel, use your newfound resourcefulness to plot out your next journey.

Say you pull out a map and decide *'Heck, South America looks cool... what if I was to motorbike from Colombia to Tierra Del Fuego...'*

Well guess what. You've travelled the world. You now know that this doesn't have to be some day time fantasy. You are a visionary, a go-getter, a 'never going to quit' adventure machine who turns dreams into a reality. Create the plan. Make the money you need. Utilize your new skills, and ditch your desk once more...

"Twenty years from now you will be more disappointed by the things you didn't do than by the ones you did do." – Mark Twain

Thanks for Reading Amigo!

The end of this book marks the beginning of your journey. From here, it's all up to you!

If you've made it this far, the only question is *when and where* are you going to travel first?

The jungles of Colombia? The temples of Myanmar? Maybe you're thinking about surfing the beaches of Indonesia, or hitchhiking across India. Trekking in Patagonia? Perhaps your **dream** is to just wander the earth, and breathe in life. To grab it by the horns and experience as much as you can whilst you figure stuff out and work out what really makes you tick...

We've covered everything you need to know to make these **dreams** a reality. And at the end of the day, your life *is* your reality, and you can make it as awesome and as rewarding as you deserve.

Your story, your destiny, is yours alone. Make it a good one.

On my own travels, I realised that I could have whatever I wanted as long as I was prepared to work for it. Hard work, and lots of it, will get you wherever you need to be.

Whatever it is you want to see. Wherever you wish to go.

Do it... The time has come to hit the road.

Travel Resources

General Awesome Resources

- The Broke Backpacker – Travel Resources Page
  www.thebrokebackpacker.com/travel-resources

- Ditch Your Desk – Learn to Make Money Online
  www.ditchyourdesk.com

- Hitchwiki – crowdsourced hitchhiking information
  www.hitchwiki.org/en/Main_Page

- Reddit Backpacking - (80,000 active members) -
  www.reddit.com/r/backpacking

- Price of Travel – Worldwide travel budgets -
  www.priceoftravel.com

Backpacking Gear

- How to Choose Your Backpack
  www.thebrokebackpacker.com/best-travel-backpack

- Always Pack a Headtorch -
  www.thebrokebackpacker.com/the-5-best-
  headlamps-for-travelling

- Picking a Tent to Take Backpacking - www.thebrokebackpacker.com/best-backpacking-tent

- Travelling with a Backpacking Stove - www.thebrokebackpacker.com/best-backpacking-stove-for-2017

- Books to Read on the Road - www.thebrokebackpacker.com/best-books-to-read-while-travelling

- Adventure Packing List - www.thebrokebackpacker.com/adventure-packing-list

Accommodation on the Road

- Couchsurfing – My secret weapon www.couchsurfing.com

- HostelWorld – My favourite hostel search engine - www.hostelworld.com

- AirBnB - www.airbnb.com (good for those special date nights – go to tinyurl.com/zf6fm83 for $35 free credit.

Work Exchanges & Volunteering

- WWOOF – www.wwoof.net/ (Organic farm work for free food and lodging)

- HelpX - www.helpx.net/ (Work in exchange for lodging and sometimes food)

- Workaway - www.workaway.info (Similar to HelpX but newer and a much better layout)

Language Learning

- uTalk - (Great format, free first phrases, good for language introduction) – www.utalkgo.com

- Fluent in 3 Months - www.fluentin3months.com

Visas

- Visa HQ - Can sort visas to tricky countries www.visahq.com

Staying Safe on the Road

- World Nomads - Get a quote here: www.worldnomads.com

- Travel Safety 101 -
  www.thebrokebackpacker.com/how-to-travel-safely

- How to Hide Money When Travelling -
  www.thebrokebackpacker.com/how-to-hide-your-money-when-travelling

Dedications

Putting together this book took over my life for about six months. This is nine years of know-how and I hope that this arms the next generation of wanderers with the tools they need to make their path that little bit clearer. Putting together something like this is no easy feat and I want to say a huge thank you to the people who encouraged me to finally sit down and write this book.

To Nina, and to my brother Alex - your support makes anything achievable.

To Aaron, my good friend - a huge thanks for your unwavering support, editing skills and brainstorming enthusiasm to help me hone this book into something that I can be proud of.

And lastly, to you - thanks for buying this book and thanks for supporting my journey, I hope to catch you on the road for a beer sometime.

Cheers,
    Will

Notes

Notes